20 Mini, Midi and Max day trip adventures around Edinburgh for all the family (including the dog)

These tried-and-tested day trips will have your family *begging* you for another outdoor adventure.

Sally & Dan Weatherly

With additional contributions from our Co-Chief Adventurers
Megan & Cole Weatherly

MEET THE TEAM

We are a family of four living in Edinburgh. We try and get out for a long walk or cycle most weekends and have put this book together to share some of our adventures (and to spare others the pain of planning).

This book portrays us to be a super fit family whose kids don't complain about going for walks.... this is not true. Sally has an aversion to any form of exercise that may involve sweating and, given the choice, our kids would happily sit on their screens all day. Dan is the Chief Adventurer (and Photographer) who researches and plans our trips.

We've definitely had adventures that have not lived up to expectations and they have not been included in this book. Through trial and error, we've found 20 mini, midi and max adventures that our whole family easily completed and enjoyed. We hope you enjoy these too.

P.S. *Yes.* We have used chocolate bars as an incentive to get to the top.

The publishers assert their right to use *Edinburgh Adventures* as a trademark of GradePod Publishing

Edinburgh Adventures
20 Mini, Midi and Max day trip adventures around Edinburgh for all the family (including the dog)

First published in the United Kingdom in 2022 by
GradePod Publishing
1A/1 Inverleith Terrace
Edinburgh
EH3 5NS

www.edinburghadventures.com

A catalogue record of this book is available from the British Library.
ISBN: 978-1-7396101-0-4 (Paperback)
ISBN: 978-1-7396101-1-1 (Hardback)

Design & Artwork: Sally Weatherly
Researched and Written by: Sally & Dan Weatherly
All photographs © Dan Weatherly
Adventurers:
- Sally, Dan, Megan & Cole Weatherly
- Jacqueline, Neil, Carmen & Eli McDonald
- Rebecca, Martha & Cormac Begley
- Ian Mackay & Jo Scott

The publishers and authors have done their best to ensure accuracy of all information in *Edinburgh Adventures*, however, they can accept no responsibility for any injury, loss, or inconvenience sustained by anyone as a result of the information or advice contained in this book.

INTRODUCTION

Find Adventure   07
Starting Points:
        Mini   10
        Midi   12
        Max   14

MINI ADVENTURES

Colinton Tunnel   16

Forth Road Bridge   22

Nine Mile Burn   28

Cramond Island   34

Cammo Estate   40

Aberlady Nature Reserve   46

MIDI ADVENTURES

St. Abbs Head   52

Twin Law Cairns   58

Abbey St. Bathans   64

Fife Coastal Route   70

West Lomond Hill   76

Innerleithen to Peebles   82

Holy Island (Lindisfarne)   88

Loch Leven   94

MAX ADVENTURES

Loch Katrine   100

The Cobbler   106

One Day: West Highland   112
Way

Rannoch Moor   118

Ben A'an   124

Corrour to Rannoch   130

TOP TIPS

Picnics and Pringles   137

FAQs   138

Get Outside

Maybe your dog is looking up at you with those begging eyes saying, "walk....?"

Maybe you're like us and spent the pandemic trying to work while simultaneously limiting kids screen time, dragging them out for walks and getting bored of the same old routes. It was **not** an adventure...

We're all more aware of the benefits of getting outside for our physical and mental health. We know we need to **Get** Outside.

It's not as simple as **"Get** Outside**"** *though - is it?*

- It takes effort to find somewhere 'different'
- The kids will complain that's it's too far / too boring / too windy...
- You're too busy to research new places

This book will help you **Get** Outside as easily as possible - helping you create an adventure to remember forever.

Outside is Free

It's hard to ignore the rapidly increasing cost of living. A one hour session in an infection-ridden soft play is the LAST thing you want to spend your hard-earned money on....

Outside is free. *Outside can also be really boring - if you don't have a plan.*

It's easier just to pay for cinema, soft play and trampoline parks.

If you choose to embark on some of the adventures in this book, we promise that costs will be minimal. **Outside is** Free, but petrol and public transport are not! We have reduced costs on every adventure by bringing picnics; however, we're suckers for a decent independent cafe and try to include a recommendation in every adventure.

This book will show you how to easily find a (*nearly!*) free adventure.

Find Freedom

We don't have a dog (much to our daughter's disgust!) but there's an unwritten rule that you need to exercise them twice a day - *right?*

It's the same with people.

If you get outside as much as possible, you **Find** Freedom that you never knew existed.

Our experience is that our kids seem to argue less when we're outside and they're not constantly asking to use the iPad. Instead, they're building little dams in rivers, climbing trees and spotting wildlife.

We live in a city centre flat. We can't just let our kids out on the street to **Find** Freedom there, but we want them to experience the adventure of childhood.

This book really tells the story of us trying to **Find** Freedom ourselves and explore the outdoors. Maybe you want that story for yourself too?

Find Adventure

We've always loved The Goonies, believing it to be the ultimate family adventure film. Imagine having that adventure in your childhood?

Whilst we can't offer our kids murdering baddies and pirate's gold, we *can* help them **Find** Adventure in their lives and make every weekend memorable.

Finding wholesome and exciting adventures is not easy, especially when so many of the tourist spots around Edinburgh are 'old news' to families who live here. Who wants to go to the National Museum of Scotland AGAIN??!!

We've put this book together to share some of our favourite day trips that are slightly more adventurous.

Find Adventure inside this book. Choose from Mini, Midi or Max adventures and make memories this weekend.

MINI ADVENTURES | STAY CLOSE

Mini adventures are great for young families, everyday dog walkers and those looking to enjoy a sunny day in Edinburgh. They are all easy, relatively flat, accessible on public transport and around 5km long.

1 **Colinton Tunnel**   p16

Celebrate Culture with Scotland's Largest Mural in Colinton Tunnel.

2 **Forth Road Bridge**   p22

Cross the 47th longest suspension bridge in the world.

3 **Nine Mile Burn**   p28

The feel of the Highlands on Edinburgh's doorstep.

4 **Cramond Island**   p34

Beat the tide and explore the World War II fortifications.

5 **Cammo Estate**   p40

Explore the ruins of Cammo Estate and see "Rapunzel's Tower"!

6 **Aberlady Nature Reserve**   p46

Sunken submarines in the sand

MIDI ADVENTURES | BRANCH OUT

Midi adventures are for those who want to branch out and explore different areas within one hour drive of Edinburgh. They are all easy, only slightly hilly, varied landscapes and between 5km to 10km long.

7 **St. Abbs Head** p52

Lighthouse, Sea Bird Colonies and a Mysterious Head in the Rocks.

8 **Twin Law Cairns** p58

Visit the Saxon Battleground between two estranged twins.

9 **Abbey St. Bathans** p64

Explore Edin's Hall Broch and cross a wobbly suspension bridge.

10 **Fife Coastal Route** p70

Explore a Hermit's cave on the coastal route from Crail to St. Monans.

11 **West Lomond Hill** p76

Dare you leap onto the mushroom-shaped Bunnet Stane?

12 **Innerleithen to Peebles** p82

A scary tunnel, ruined castle and a daredevil's pump track

13 **Holy Island (Lindisfarne)** p88

Embrace the mud on this easy causeway walk across Pilgrim's Way.

14 **Loch Leven** p94

Flat, traffic-free, gravel path along the heritage trail circling Loch Leven.

MAX ADVENTURES | TRUE EXPLORATION

Max adventures are not difficult, but each have their own special feature making it a day you'll never forget. Most starting points are a couple of hours drive from Edinburgh and will require an early start, or an overnight stay.

15 **Loch Katrine**   p100

Board the Sir Walter Scott Steam Boat with your bike and cycle back.

16 **The Cobbler**   p106

The drama of the Arrochar Alps and the famous Cobbler.

17 **One Day: West Highland Way**   p112

From Crianlarich to Bridge of Orchy.

18 **Rannoch Moor**   p118

Follow the Military Road landing in the jaws of Glencoe.

19 **Ben A'an**   p124

A mountain in miniature, with outstanding views of the Trossachs.

20 **Corrour to Rannoch**   p130

Get the Trainspotting vibe on the Road to the Isles

Colinton Tunnel

Mini Adventure

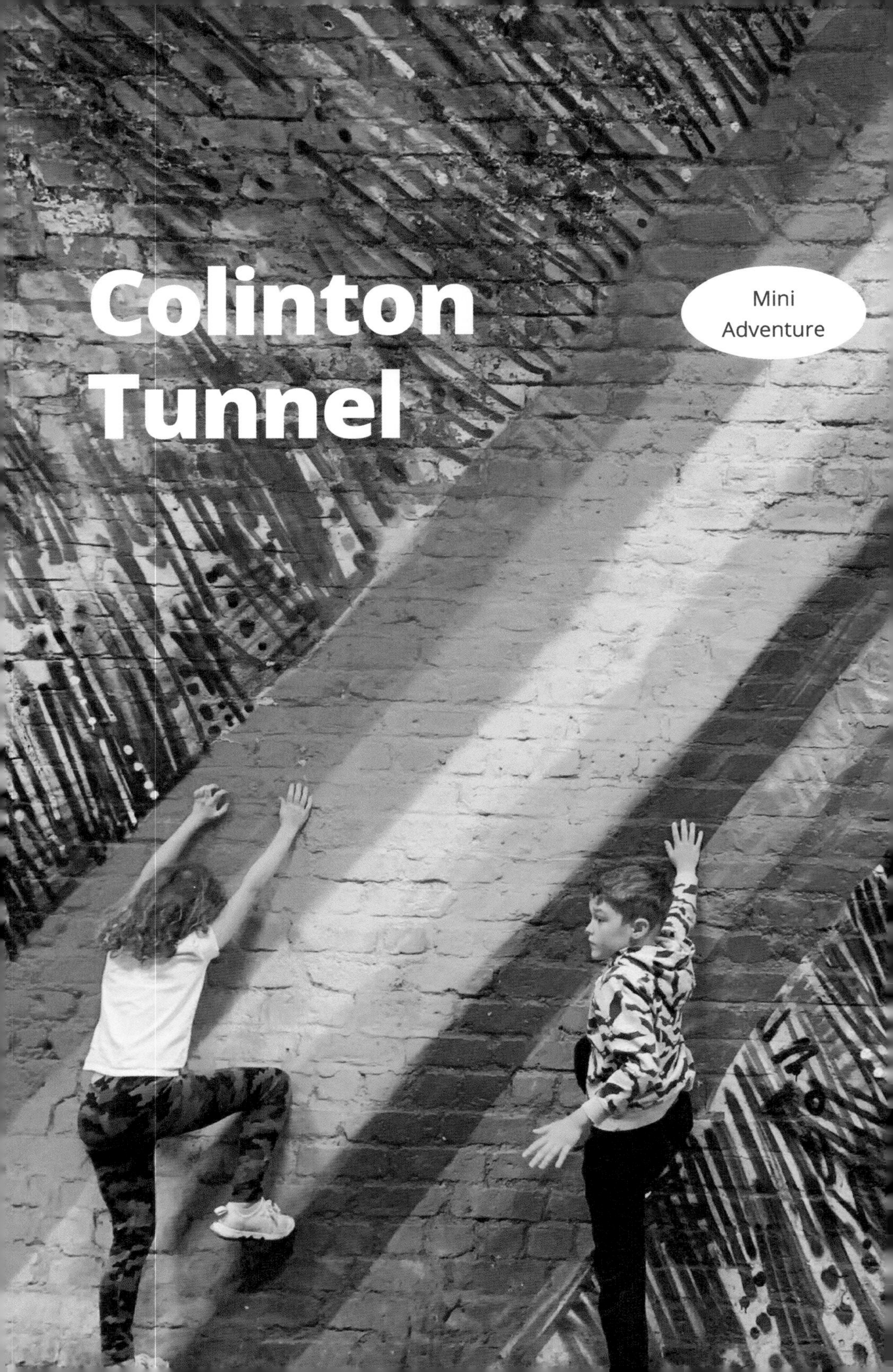

COLINTON TUNNEL

MINI ADVENTURE

SUMMARY

Walk from the City Centre to celebrate culture with Scotland's largest mural inside a formerly derelict Colinton Tunnel, featuring local art and Robert Louis Stevenson's poem 'A view from a railway carriage'

START POINT

📍 EH3 9BA

🚌 Lothian Buses No's. 10, 45 and 16

🅿 Free Street Parking in Bruntsfield

📱 Scan below to download route

Difficulty	Easy
Distance	6 km
Location	Edinburgh
Walk Type	A → B
Ascent	76 metres
What to Pack	Trainers, Water bottle, Bus fare

RATINGS

Scenery

Fun Factor

Dog Suitability

Public Toilets

GETTING TO THE START

This adventure stays in Edinburgh (and involves getting the bus....)

Kids in Edinburgh are entitled to free bus travel until they are 21. This walk could be the catalyst you need to get their bus passes organised. Just search "Young Person's Free Bus Travel Scheme". The form is pretty straightforward.

The walk starts at the mouth of the Union Canal in Fountainbridge, Edinburgh Quay
(POSTCODE: EH3 9BA)

If you are driving to the start, then save the hefty city centre parking fees and find a parking space in nearby Bruntsfield. You can join the canal path from there. Also... the bus from Colinton will bring you back to Bruntsfield - so that's useful.

SPECIAL NOTES

You'll have to get the bus back from Colinton to City Centre at the end. Best to check ahead to make sure the buses are running.

HIGHLIGHTS

- At the start of the walk, on the Union Canal, there's a little blue canal barge that has been brought back to life as a floating coffee shop. You can pick up some refreshments here - if needed.
- The landscape changes with each kilometre, as you walk down the canal, along the Water of Leith and finally into the Colinton Tunnel.
- There are a couple of nice pubs near Colinton Tunnel that might help round off the day in a merry way!

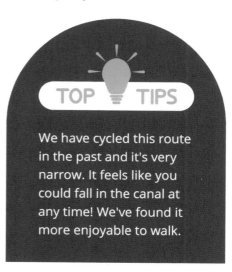

TOP TIPS

We have cycled this route in the past and it's very narrow. It feels like you could fall in the canal at any time! We've found it more enjoyable to walk.

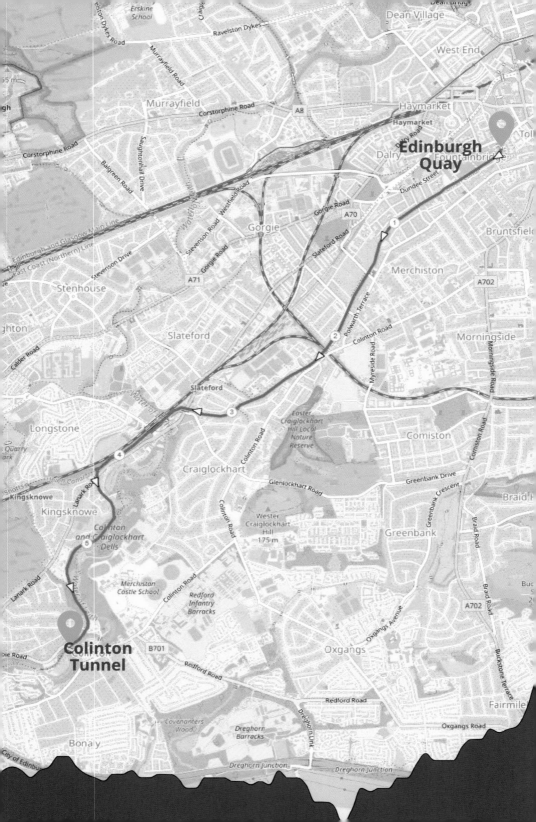

WALK DESCRIPTION

1 The Union Canal is found behind a bunch of new, office-looking buildings in Fountainbridge! It's behind the Quay 2 buildings.

2 Stay on the right hand side of the canal, with the mural boards on your right hand side. You'll quickly see the cafe barge and the Leamington Lift Bridge.

3 Follow the path with the canal on your left. After about 2 miles, you'll arrive at the Slateford Aqueduct, which you'll walk over.

4 Shortly after the Slateford Aqueduct, you'll start to think about leaving the canal path onto the Water of Leith - towards Colinton Dell. It's quite easy to miss this turn off to the left so look out for a footbridge that goes up and over to the left of the union canal path.

5 This new path follows the Water of Leith and into Colinton Dell - a truly lovely part of the world.

6 Eventually you'll reach the highlight (and the end) of your walk - the Colinton Tunnel. It's a colourful and exciting art project that really has brought this old Victorian tunnel to life.

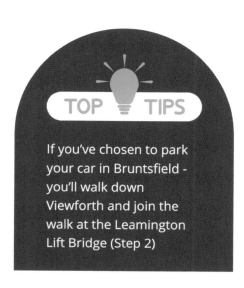

TOP TIPS

If you've chosen to park your car in Bruntsfield - you'll walk down Viewforth and join the walk at the Leamington Lift Bridge (Step 2)

Forth Road Bridge

SUMMARY

Cross over to the Kingdom of Fife at a height of 110m on the 47th longest suspension bridge in the world. Finish off your walk with some crabbing under the famous rail bridge

START POINT

📍 EH30 9SF

🚌 Lothian Country 43

🅿 Free Parking at Visitor Centre

📱 Scan below to download route

FORTH ROAD BRIDGE

MINI ADVENTURE

Difficulty	Easy
Distance	5 km
Location	South Queensferry
Walk Type	There and back
Ascent	24 metres
What to Pack	Water bottle Snacks Crabbing Kit

RATINGS

Scenery	▬▬▬
Fun Factor	▬▬▬
Dog Suitability	▬▬▬
Public Toilets	▬▬▬

GETTING TO THE START

The footpath over the Forth Road Bridge starts at the car park beside the Forth Bridges Contact and Education Centre (POSTCODE: EH30 9SF). Drive passed the petrol station after turning left at the roundabout and you'll see a large car park in front of you. The car park has a little picnic kiosk and a viewpoint to enjoy before embarking on your journey.

There are plenty of East Coast Stagecoach buses (X55, X58, X59, X60) and a Lothian Country Bus (43) that will take you near to the starting point. It takes about 25-40 minutes to travel there from Edinburgh city centre.

CRABBING

Take a crab line, crabbing bucket and some smoked bacon. Head to Hawes Pier or Whitehouse Bay after your walk for some crabbing.

Slack water (the time around **high or low tide**) is the best time to crab.

HIGHLIGHTS

- Take a moment to look at the thousands of romantic padlocks attached to the central panels of the bridge; a practice which began in 2014 to raise thousands of pounds for the RNLI Queensferry Lifeboat Station.

- The height of the crossing over the water results in spectacular views of the Forth as well as the bridges.

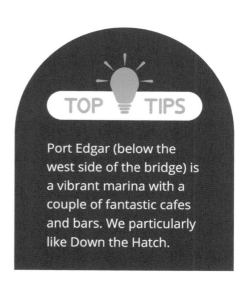

TOP TIPS

Port Edgar (below the west side of the bridge) is a vibrant marina with a couple of fantastic cafes and bars. We particularly like Down the Hatch.

Hawes Pier (Good Crabbing!)

Forth Bridge Visitor Centre Car Park

WALK DESCRIPTION

The Forth Road Bridge was the fourth longest in the world when it opened in 1964. In total, the structure is over 2.5 km long. Oh... and it's always windy - pack a warm jumper!

1. Take a moment to visit the view point in the car park, detailing some interesting landmarks before you start the walk.

2. From the car park, pass to the left of the toilets, and down steps to reach the footpath on the near side of the dual carriageway across the bridge.

3. Turn right along the footpath out onto the Forth Road Bridge. Most walkers would use the East path across the bridge, but you can use the underpass if you prefer walking over the west side.

4. The path rises gently as it climbs towards the first of the support towers. After passing the mid point, the bridge levels off and you'll see the love lock panels.

5. After passing the second tower, the walkway leads downhill towards the Fife side of the bridge. Return the way you came after you feel you've walked far enough!

TOP TIPS

If the Contact and Education Centre is open (situated in the car park), the lovely staff there will give your kids some activity packs to complete on the crossing.

27

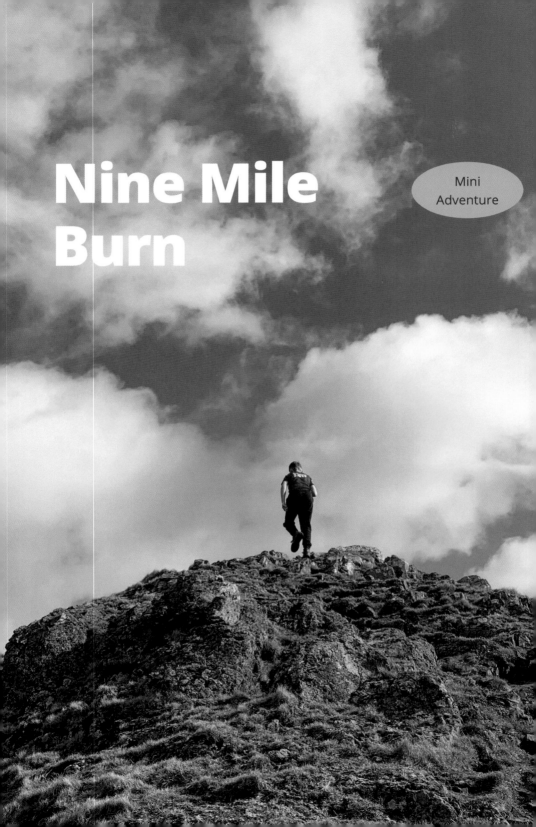

Nine Mile Burn

Mini Adventure

NINE MILE BURN

MINI ADVENTURE

SUMMARY

Away from the Pentland crowds, this relatively unknown walk has the 'feel' of the Highlands and gets you up one of the highest peaks in the Pentlands without really noticing.

START POINT

📍	EH26 9LZ
🚌	Stagecoach No. 101
🅿️	Free Parking on Roman Road
📱	Scan below to download route

Difficulty	Easy
Distance	6-7 km
Location	Pentlands
Walk Type	Circular
Ascent	300 metres
What to Pack	Hiking boots Water bottle Picnic

RATINGS

Scenery

Fun Factor

Dog Suitability

Public Toilets

Sheep Grazing Area
Please keep your dog
on a short lead
or close at heel

GETTING TO THE START

Don't worry! We're **NOT** going to tell you to drive to the Pentlands and park at the Flotterstone... We've all been there (and our car was broken into!). For this walk you need to drive a little further until you reach the small hamlet of Nine Mile Burn adjacent to the A702. Turn right off the A702 (just after the abandoned Aston Martin garage).

There is a small row of free car parking paces (enough for around 20 cars) in the small hamlet of Nine Mile Burn.

Stagecoach Buses also runs an hourly bus service which stops at Nine Mile Burn (either the 101 to Biggar or 102 to Dumfries). It takes under 45 minutes from the Bus Station in central Edinburgh and is around £5 return.

WILDLIFE WATCH

It's a ground nesting site for skylark, curlew and merlin. Dogs should be kept on a lead.

HIGHLIGHTS

- We've done this walk with four different families (and dogs). We've walked in the snow and in the summer. It's been a success every time.
- The best thing about the Nine Mile Burn is that you get to the top of West Kip without really noticing. It's a good starter hillwalk for little kids and small dogs.
- A perfect way to see the beautiful peaks of the surrounding Pentland hills.

TOP TIPS

It's tempting to skip out the short, steep drag up to the top of West Kip. Trust us... it'll be over quickly and the views are really worth it!

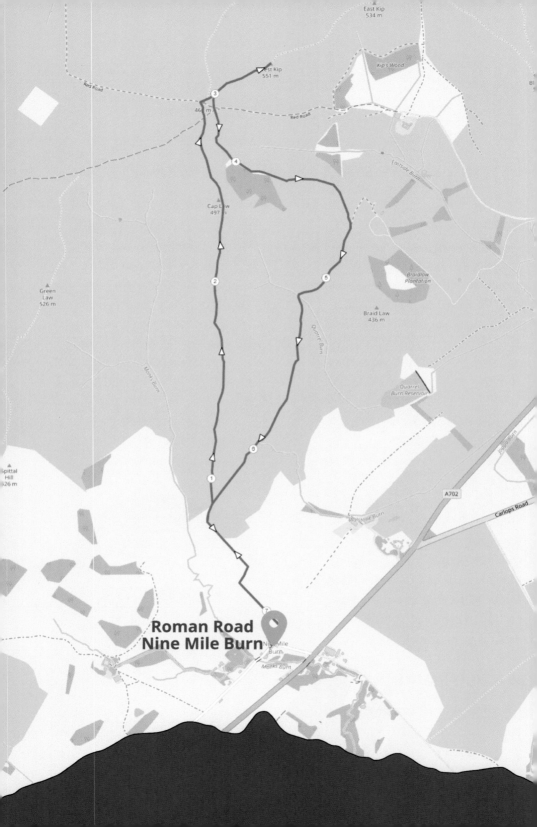

**Roman Road
Nine Mile Burn**

WALK DESCRIPTION

West Kip (the 3,477th highest hill in Scotland!) makes for a fine point to aim for on this walk and its narrow outline is quite different to the rounded shapes of other hills surrounding it.

1. Go through the gate out of the car park into the field ahead of you and walk uphill parallel to the stone wall.

2. At the top of the field there is a stile on the right hand side to cross with a sign to Monks Rigg.

3. Follow the path to Monks Rigg which continues uphill and opens up into moorland. The views behind you open up to the Moorfoot Hills and ahead of you the sharp outline of West Kip starts to come into view.

4. Once at the foot of West Kip you can see the Forth Road bridges in the distance. From here take the clearly defined steep path up to the top of West Kip. The climb is short and sharp but over quickly.

5. Once at the top of West Kip enjoy views of the stunning ridge line across to East Kip. Descend the way you came.

6. At the bottom of West Kip, bear left and follow the path at the bottom of the treeline. The path is well defined and signposted at several points to Nine Mile Burn. You finally end up at the top of the field back to the car park.

TOP TIPS

This walk is especially fun when it snows. Take a sledge.

33

Cramond Island

Mini Adventure

CRAMOND ISLAND

SUMMARY

Beat the tide at Cramond Island and explore the World War 2 structures dotted across the island.

START POINT

📍 EH4 6NU

🚌 Lothian Bus No. 41

🅿 Free Parking at Cramond Village car park

📱 Scan below to download route

Difficulty	Easy
Distance	3-4km
Location	Edinburgh
Walk Type	There and back
Ascent	29 metres
Time	2-3 hours

RATINGS

Scenery	▬▬▬
Fun Factor	▬▬▬▬
Dog Suitability	▬▬▬
Public Toilets	▬▬▬

GETTING TO THE START

The Cramond promenade is easily accessible by bike using the Edinburgh cycle network.

The 41 bus takes you to Cramond village and the 29 takes you to Silverknowes.

If you are driving then there is plenty of parking on Marine Drive or at the car park in Cramond village (POSTCODE: EH4 6NU)

SPECIAL NOTE

Cross the causeway at low tide.

Safe crossing time can be found displayed on the board at the Cramond Village car park or by texting the word Cramond to 81400

HIGHLIGHTS

- Explore Cramond Island and its WW2 buildings.
- Walk the promenade between Silverknowes and Cramond (great place to cycle or rollerblade as it's lovely and wide).
- Enjoy an ice cream from the van at the start of the causeway.

The causeway is really impressive with WWII concrete pylons running its length.

TOP TIPS

Leave enough time to explore the island without having to rush back. There are loads of empty buildings to explore.

Cramond Village Car Park

WALK DESCRIPTION

1 Start anywhere along the Cramond Promenade! It's probably easiest to start in the Cramond Village car park (the information board for the tide is there).

2 Head towards the line of triangular concrete posts alongside the causeway - easily visible from the promenade.

3 There is a tricky bit getting from the jetty down onto the walkway. The walk over the causeway takes longer than you might think, especially if your kids are like ours and inspect every rock pool in great detail!

4 Enjoy the island at your leisure. Lots of old fortifications to explore and great views from the top of the small hill.

5 Make sure you get back before the tide come in!

TOP TIPS

Bring a picnic. We've found the cafes and pubs in the immediate area surrounding the island to be very expensive. Anyway... who doesn't love a beach picnic?!

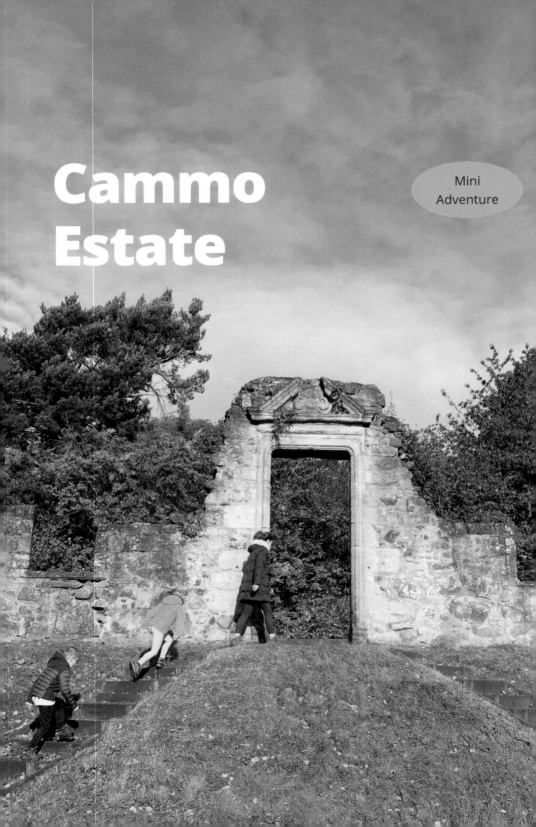

Cammo Estate

Mini Adventure

CAMMO ESTATE

SUMMARY

Cammo Estate is a fun adventure at all times of the year. It doesn't take all day. There's lots to explore and if you're lucky you'll find a tree swing for the "kids" to play on.

START POINT

📍 EH4 8AN

🚌 Lothian Country No.43

🅿 Free Parking on Cammo Walk

📱 Scan below to download route

Difficulty	Easy
Distance	4 km
Location	Edinburgh
Walk Type	Circular
Ascent	64 metres
What to Pack	Hiking boots, or Wellies Water bottle Picnic

RATINGS

Scenery
Fun Factor
Dog Suitability
Public Toilets

GETTING TO THE START

You can access Cammo Estate by bicycle, bus, or by car at the end Cammo Road from the A90. There is a free car park on Cammo Walk. (POSTCODE: EH4 8AN)

If using public transport, catch the Lothian Country bus (No. 43) from Princes Street towards Queensferry. Buses run every 20 minutes and take about 45 minutes.

To cycle there, follow the National Cycle Route 1 from Edinburgh West End to Cramond Bridge. Cammo Estate is a short cycle from the official cycle route. Although the cycle does follow many roads, it is a safe cycle that can be done with younger children.

SPECIAL NOTES

The toilets at the visitor centre are only open every Sunday between 2-4pm.

HIGHLIGHTS

- Find Rapunzel in her tower. Sadly, "Rapunzel's Tower" is only a water tower designed to supply water to the nearby Cammo House. It looks the part though!
- There is a stunning arboretum. If you plan a visit in autumn - you won't be disappointed.
- Climb the ruins of Cammo House and its stables.
- There are many tree swings dotted throughout the estate.

TOP TIPS

We took a set of laser guns on this walk. The kids LOVED playing laser guns in the ruins of the old house.

Cammo Walk
Car Park

North Park

West Park

Home Field

East Avenue

High Park

Curling

Standing Stone

South Field

South Avenue

Walled
Garden

Cammo Estate Local Nature Reserve

Cammo
Tower

Mouseity
Hill

Cammo Road

Cammo Walk

Cammo Walk

Cammo Walk

Cammo Walk

Cammo Walk

Cammo Walk

Cammo
Lodge
Visitor
Centre

Strathalmo

1

2

3

4

WALK DESCRIPTION

Cammo House was built around 1700 and contained twenty rooms, consisting of four public rooms, smoking room, billiards room, and fourteen bedrooms. There were also bathrooms, laundry, wash-house, kitchen, pantries, larder, two lofts, two cellars, and ample servant's accommodation.

Between 1955 and 1975, the house fell into a state of disrepair. It was eventually given to the Edinburgh Council in the 1970's.

1 From the car park, follow the tree-lined avenue to the ruined stables.

2 Take this time to turn left and explore "Rapunzel's Tower" and the man-made hill beside it - for great views of Edinburgh.

3 Back to the ruined stables (game of hide and seek here?) and go straight on the path (stables on your left). This will take you to the ruined Cammo House.

4 To the north of the ruined house is a grove of five old yew tres. This area is also host to one of the oldest ash trees in the city, as well as giant redwood, cedar and Douglas fir.

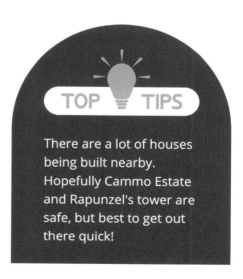

TOP TIPS

There are a lot of houses being built nearby. Hopefully Cammo Estate and Rapunzel's tower are safe, but best to get out there quick!

Aberlady Nature Reserve

Mini Adventure

ABERLADY NATURE RESERVE

SUMMARY

A stroll through a varied nature reserve, opening out onto a beach. Go at low tide to visit the submarine wrecks before climbing the cliffs and finishing in Gullane

START POINT

📍 EH32 0QB

🚌 East Coast No.124

🅿 Free Parking at Aberlady Nature Reserve

📱 Scan below to download route

Difficulty	Easy
Distance	7 km
Location	East Lothian
Walk Type	A → B
Ascent	35 metres
What to Pack	Hiking boots Water bottle Picnic Bus money

RATINGS

Scenery	▬▬▬▬▬
Fun Factor	▬▬▬▬▬
Dog Suitability	▏
Public Toilets	▬▬▬

GETTING TO THE START

Head to the car park at the entrance to Aberlady Nature Reserve (where there is a large wooden footbridge) around 1km east of Aberlady village (POSTCODE: EH32 0QB).

If using public transport, you can catch the East Coast No. 124 towards North Berwick from St Andrew's House in Edinburgh. Buses run every half an hour and take about an hour.

SPECIAL NOTES

No dogs in the nature reserve - sorry!

You'll have to get the bus back from Gullane to Aberlady at the end. Best to check ahead to make sure the buses are running.

HIGHLIGHTS

- Explore the hulks of two Second World War midget submarines on Aberlady Beach.
- Spot special wildlife on the walk through the Nature Reserve, towards the sand dunes.
- The sand dunes are super fun to play on.
- From the beach, the coastal walk to Gullane has stunning views

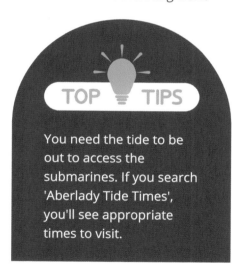

TOP TIPS

You need the tide to be out to access the submarines. If you search 'Aberlady Tide Times', you'll see appropriate times to visit.

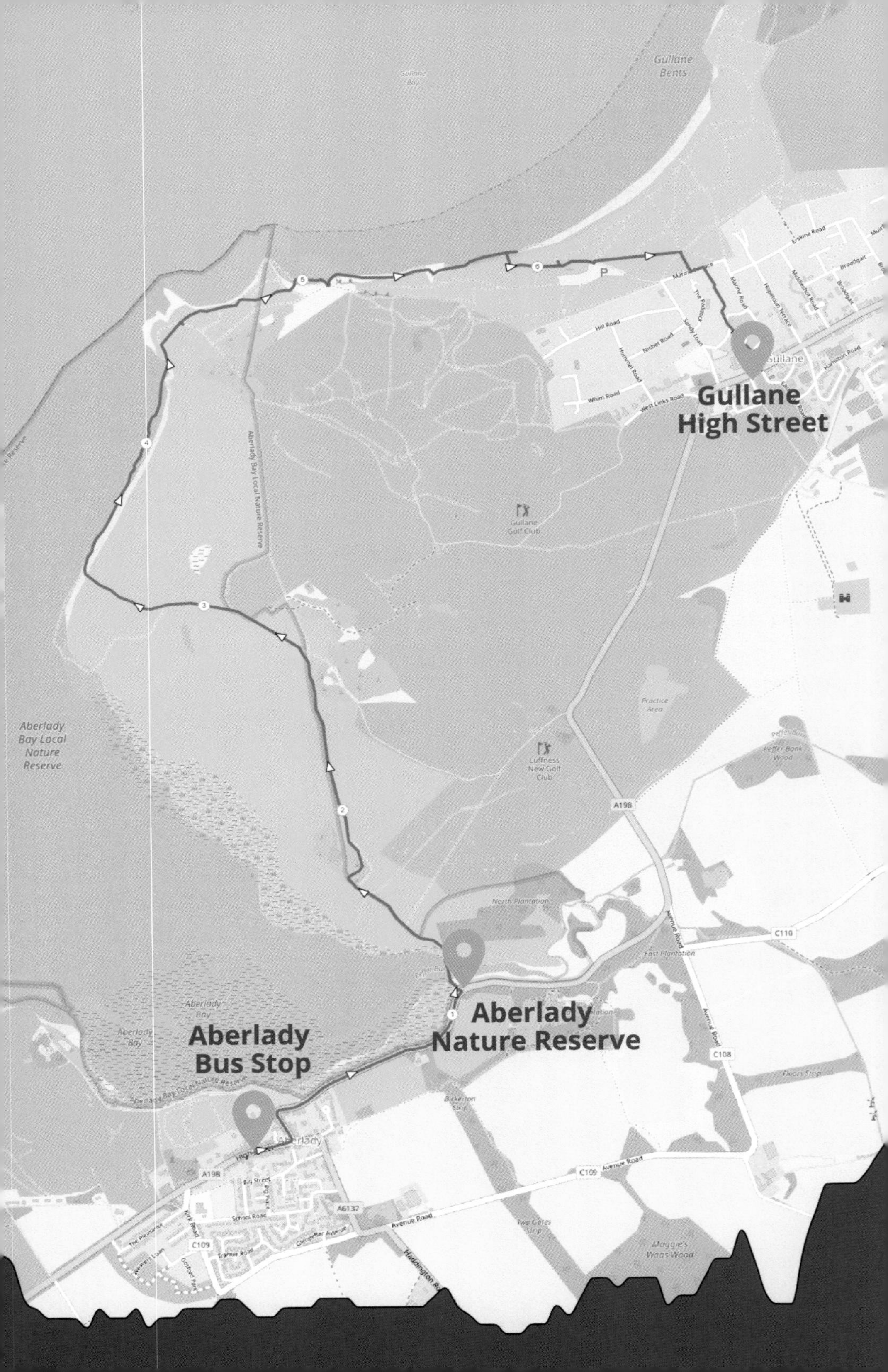

Gullane Bents
Gullane Bay
Gullane High Street
Gullane
Aberlady Nature Reserve
Aberlady Bus Stop
Aberlady
Aberlady Bay Local Nature Reserve
Aberlady Bay
Gullane Golf Club
Luffness New Golf Club
Practice Area
Peffer Bank Wood
North Plantation
East Plantation
Bickerton Strip
Two Gates Strip
Maggie's Waas Wood
Fluors Strip
Hill Road
Nisbet Road
Hummel Road
Whim Road
West Links Road
Sandy Loan
Marine Road
Erskine Road
Broadgait
Hamilton Road
Avenue Road
Haddington Road
School Road
Kirk Road
The Pleasance
A198
A6137
C109
C110
C108
1
2
3
4
5
6

WALK DESCRIPTION

1 Follow the Nature Reserve footpath out to the beach across the footbridge. You'll walk through a 'tunnel' of bushes and pass the Marl Loch on your left.

2 Turn left at the junction of paths and head towards the big sand dune. Climb this big sand dune and run down the other side! Don't worry if you get lost - just keep heading for the sea.

3 From the top of the sand dunes, you can see the submarines if you look over towards the Pentlands. To reach them, it's about a 15 minute walk (three-quarters of a mile) across the sand.

4 After visiting the submarines, turn east and continue to the far end of the beach where it becomes rockier, and take a path that heads up onto the low dunes to reach Gullane Point.

5 Follow the paths and eventually you'll see some concrete defences from the Second World War. Climb up to them. The grassy track turns to the left above the clifftops - with the golf courses of Gullane on the right. You'll have to cross one of the golf course tees at one point.

6 It's fairly straightforward to find Gullane from there!

TOP TIPS

We enjoyed some refreshments in The Old Clubhouse in Gullane before catching the bus back to Aberlady. They have outdoor seating.

St. Abbs Head

Midi
Adventure

ST. ABBS HEAD

SUMMARY

Lighthouse, seabird colonies and a mysterious head in the rocks at St. Abbs. Enjoy a leisurely picnic on the cliffs as part of this loop trail with stunning views.

START POINT

📍 TD14 5QF

🚌 Border Bus No. 235

🅿️ National Trust Pay and Display

📱 Scan below to download route

Difficulty	Easy
Distance	6-7 km
Location	St. Abbs (1 hour drive from Edinburgh)
Walk Type	Circular
Ascent	110 metres
What to Pack	Hiking boots Water bottle Picnic

RATINGS

Scenery	▬▬▬▬
Fun Factor	▬▬▬
Dog Suitability	▬▬▬
Public Toilets	▬▬▬

GETTING TO THE START

St Abbs is a one hour drive from Edinburgh along the A1. There is plenty of parking at the National Trust Reserve: **Northfield, Eyemouth, TD14 5QF.** It's a pay and display car park with parking costing £3 for all day and **free to National Trust members**.

Frustratingly, there are no buses from Edinburgh but if you take a train to Berwick Upon Tweed there is a **direct bus** to St Abbs which leaves every 90 minutes.

We've done this walk a few times and always stop on the way for coffee and pastries at **Bostock Bakery at East Linton (EH40 3DE)** just off the A1. If you haven't packed a picnic they have lots of amazing sandwiches and savoury pastries.

WILDLIFE WATCH

This nature reserve is famous for wildlife, particularly bird watching.

HIGHLIGHTS

- Veer off track a few metres (to the west of the lighthouse) and you'll see the most incredible colonies of seabirds hidden in the cliffs.
- There are truly stunning views of dramatic coastline along the whole walk.
- Lots of places for a quick paddle in the sea to cool off.
- The best picnic spot is beside the lighthouse.

TOP TIPS

Set off early and combine this trip with an afternoon at the beach at Coldingham Bay. It's a lovely sheltered beach with easy parking.

WALK DESCRIPTION

Once you arrive at St Abbs nature reserve car park, there are helpful signs showing the route. You may want to start at the Old Smiddy Cafe and use the excellent public toilets there too!

1. Walk down past the cafe, follow the road down to the stone wall and turn left towards the coast.

2. There is a gradual climb with lots of benches to stop and admire the scenery. Follow the path over the hill and back up the headland towards the lighthouse.

3. After the lighthouse, continue on the tarmac road. At the bottom of the hill (before the cattle grid), there's an old slipway for boats (Pettico Wick Harbour), just off the road on the right. You can see St. Abbs Head on the rocks from there.

4. The walk back to the car park is through lush green farmland. Follow the farm road. The coast views sadly disappear but there are lots of beautiful open fields to enjoy.

5. Towards the end of the walk, you'll approach farm buildings and holiday homes, after passing through the country gate. Keep any dogs on a lead in the farm - they'll worry the sheep.

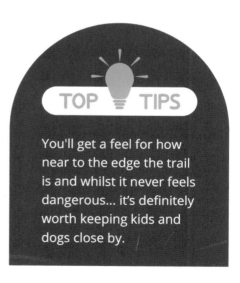

TOP TIPS

You'll get a feel for how near to the edge the trail is and whilst it never feels dangerous... it's definitely worth keeping kids and dogs close by.

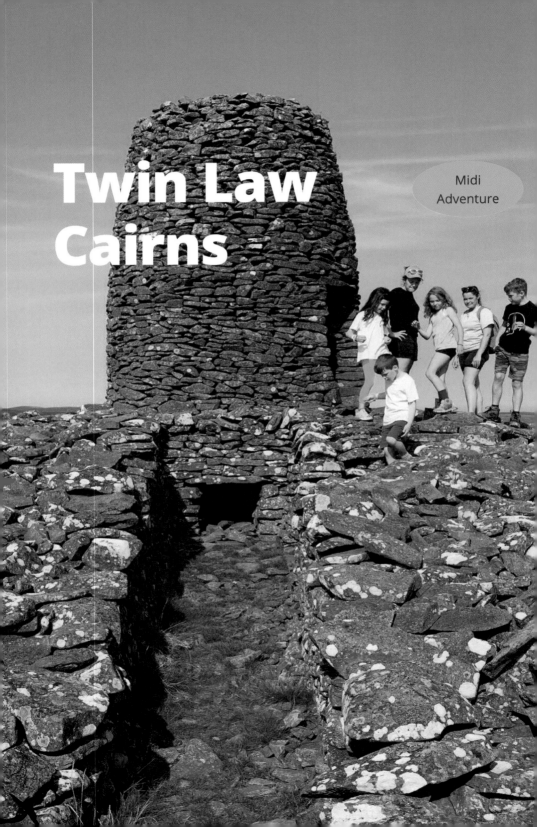

Twin Law Cairns

Midi
Adventure

TWIN LAW CAIRNS

SUMMARY

Visit a Saxon Battleground at the Twin Law Cairns, with an easy ascent on the Southern Upland Way and lots of landmarks to keep you moving.

START POINT

⦿ TD11 3PE

🏃 Southern Upland Way

🅿 Watch Water Reservoir Car Park

📱 Scan below to download route

Difficulty	Easy
Distance	10 km
Location	Longformacus (1 hour drive from Edinburgh)
Walk Type	There and back
Ascent	217 metres
What to Pack	Hiking boots Water bottle Picnic

RATINGS

Scenery	▬▬▬▬
Fun Factor	▬▬▬▬
Dog Suitability	▬▬▬
Public Toilets	▬▬▬

GETTING TO THE START

The nearest postcode is: TD11 3PE **BUT** the postcode is not the start!

Please drive to Longformacus and follow the instructions below:

As you drive from the Lammermuir hills through Longformacus (towards Duns), you'll see a small road off to the right. Turn onto that small road and you'll see the Longformacus community park on your right. You need to follow this road for about three miles. You will feel like you're driving through Rawburn Farm but keep going!

Eventually you'll see Watch Water Reservoir and the fishery building on the other side. Drive all the way to the fishery and park in the car park. It's free to park there.

HIGHLIGHTS

You'll see two interesting landmarks on this walk:

- **Dippie's Well:** The inscription reads, "there is no water on the Lammermuirs sweeter than at John Dippie's well." John Dippie was the gamekeeper on this land at one time in history and the rumour is that he stashed his whisky here!

- **Twin Law Cairns:** Two cairns built for twin brothers separated at birth, who unwittingly fought against each other (and died) in the Battle of Twinlaw in Saxon times. Read the poem dedicated to the brothers on the cairns AND there's often some treats left by other walkers in the little metal box. Why not leave a treat for others there too.

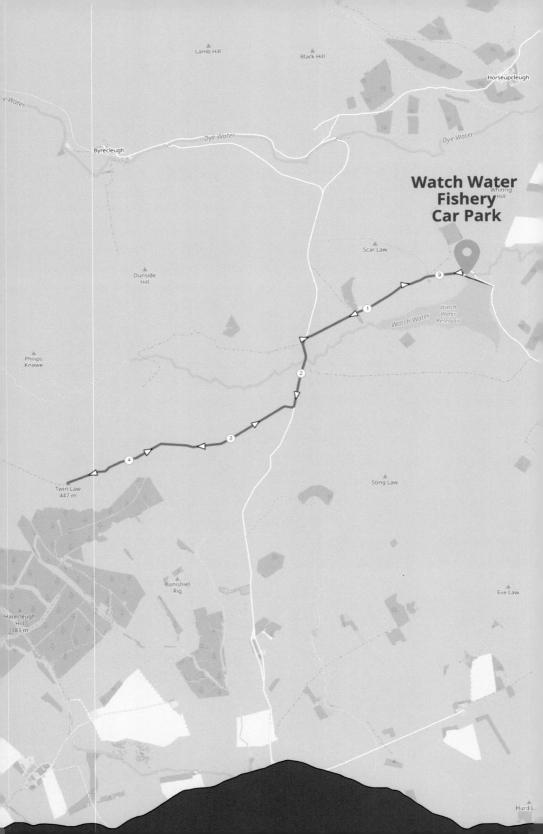

Watch Water Fishery Car Park

Horseupcleugh

Lamb Hill

Black Hill

Dye Water

Dye Water

Byrecleugh

Whinrig Hill

Scar Law

Dunside Hill

Watch Water

Watch Water Reservoir

Philips Knowe

Sting Law

Twin Law 447 m

Eve Law

Banishiel Rig

Harecleugh Hill 383 m

Hurd L.

WALK DESCRIPTION

Park at the Watch Water Reservoir Fishery car park. The fishery has toilets and light refreshments, but hasn't been open on our last couple of visits. However, the outdoor picnic benches at the fishery are great for a picnic before you start.

1 Leave the fishery car park and turn left. Follow the farm road, passing lots of sheep, some farm buildings and a small ford.

2 Eventually you'll reach a t-junction and you'll turn left down the hill towards the small river in the valley.

3 Just before the river, on the right hand side, look out for Dippie's Well. The kids can have a play on the bridges there too. Dogs can cool off in the river!

4 Follow the road up the hill until you see a sign off to the right for the Southern Upland Way. Follow this path all the way up the hill, with the fence on your left. Eventually, you'll cross a style over the wall and it's the final push to the twin cairns.

5 Return the way you came.

TOP TIPS

The last time we did this walk, we managed to fit in a swim at a nearby loch! Drive to Whiteadder reservoir, which is about 20 minutes away. There's a pier that you can jump off and some fantastic spots for a BBQ.

63

Abbey St. Bathans

Midi Adventure

ABBEY ST. BATHANS

SUMMARY

A circular walk climbing Cockburn Law, exploring Edin's Hall Broch, crossing the wobbly Elba suspension bridge and savouring the baked goods at the Riverside Bakehouse.

START POINT

- 📍 TD11 3TX
- Southern Upland Way
- Ⓟ Abbey St. Bathans (free)
- Scan below to download route

Difficulty	Easy
Distance	11 km
Location	Abbey St. Bathans (1 hour drive from Edinburgh)
Walk Type	Circular
Ascent	323 metres
What to Pack	Walking boots Water bottle Picnic

RATINGS

Scenery	
Fun Factor	
Dog Suitability	
Public Toilets	

GETTING TO THE START

This walk starts in the beautiful little village of Abbey St. Bathans (TD11 3TX) in the Lammermuir district of the Borders.

It takes around an hour to drive there from Edinburgh and there's a sizeable free car park in the village. The car park is the starting point for a numbers of walks; the Southern Upland Way passes through this point.

This walk is a circular walk, which heads away from the Riverside Bakehouse, with the river on your left.

Sadly, there are no public transport services to Abbey St. Bathans.

HIGHLIGHTS

- **Cockburn Law:** There is a hill-fort on its summit, which is surrounded by two concentric ramparts. The views are fantastic.
- **Edin's Hall Broch:** There is some controversy around this broch, with some suggesting it could be a roundhouse because of its huge radius of 11m. Nevertheless, it's a lovely place for a picnic and a rest!
- **Whiteadder Water Suspension Bridge:** The walk directs you across this suspension footbridge, warning you that only two people should cross at any one time. There's definitely an "Indiana Jones" feel to this bridge!
- **The Riverside Bakehouse:** This cafe is situated at the car park and serves light lunches, coffees and delicious artisan cakes. We had a cruffin (cross between a croissant and a muffin!) and it was something else...

Abbey St. Bathans
Car Park

WALK DESCRIPTION

1 From the Riverside Bakehouse car park, head down the footpath with the river on your left and under the telegraph poles. You'll quickly meet a minor road then follow another path off to the left after the woodyard.

2 You rejoin the road, turn left and follow the road until you see a sign saying "TOOT" on a sharp bend. Take the footpath on this bend, cross the river and climb up the contours of an open field.

3 Stay on this path until you reach the signposts. You'll return to this point later. Turn right to head towards Cockburn Law, following sheep paths through the gorse. Head towards the top of the hill!

4 Once at the top, retrace your steps back down to the footpath junction with the sign. Now go straight ahead following the direction of Edin's Hall Broch.

5 After the broch, head east and the path slopes down to reach a kissing gate above woodland on the left. Follow the perimeter of a field and you'll see a gap in the bushes, leading through someone's private garden. Keep following the signs and you'll cross the suspension bridge.

6 After the suspension bridge, you'll meet a narrow road. Turn right up that road and follow it until you meet a t-junction. Take a left up the hill for 1.5km and then first right.

7 Continue straight ahead onto an unsurfaced track and follow signs for Abbey St. Bathans.

Fife Coastal Route

Midi
Adventure

SUMMARY

Explore a Hermit's cave on the coastal route from Crail to St. Monans. It's a stunning coastal walk from, with stops for cave exploration, fish and chips and shell collecting

START POINT

📍 Crail

🚌 East Scotland No. 95

🅿️ St. Monans, free street parking

📱 Scan below to download route

FIFE COASTAL ROUTE

MIDI ADVENTURE

Difficulty	Easy
Distance	12 km
Location	St. Monans (1 hour drive from Edinburgh)
Walk Type	A → B
Ascent	77 metres
What to Pack	Hiking boots Water bottle Snacks Bus Fare

RATINGS

Scenery	▬▬▬▬▬
Fun Factor	▬▬▬▬▬
Dog Suitability	▬▬▬▬
Public Toilets	▬▬▬▬

GETTING TO THE START

It's just under an hour to drive to St. Monans from Edinburgh. Once you arrive, you'll notice that parking is free in the village. Just be mindful of where you've parked - so you don't block anything on the harbour!

Catch the No. 95 bus to Crail from the main road (A917), which is just a short walk up from the harbour. You'll see the bus shelter. The bus leaves just before every hour (i.e. 09:53am, 10:53am, etc) and takes 32 minutes. So you'll probably want to catch the 9:53am bus in St. Monans. This may seem like an early start, but I PROMISE it's worth it!

If you don't have a car then St. Monans can be accessed by bus from Edinburgh. Stagecoach East Scotland operates a bus from West End, Queensferry Street to St Monans, Station Road every 3 hours. Tickets cost £8 - £13 and the journey takes 2h 3m.

HIGHLIGHTS

- Park in St. Monans and easily get the bus to Crail.
- Stunning 4 mile walk from Crail to Anstruther (1.5-2 hours) along the Fife Coastal Trail, exploring caves and ruins en route.
- Fish and Chips in Anstruther for lunch.
- Another easy 3 mile walk from Anstruther to St. Monans (1-1.5 hours).
- Watch the sun set over the harbour in St. Monans and find your car!

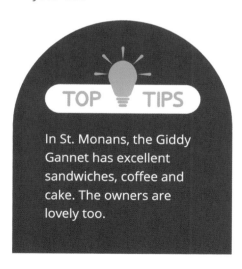

TOP TIPS

In St. Monans, the Giddy Gannet has excellent sandwiches, coffee and cake. The owners are lovely too.

WALK DESCRIPTION

After getting off the bus from St. Monans, keep an eye out for Fife Coastal Trail signs. You're going to follow this path for 4 miles and it will take around 1.5 - 2 hours.

1 The walk follows the coast, passing some truly fantastic places to explore. The first cool place is the Caves of Caiplie, known locally as The Coves. You can explore inside AND climb (safely) up on top of them from behind.

2 You'll arrive in Anstruther (probably hungry!) and there are lots of places to eat. We usually bring a picnic, but knew we wanted fish and chips in Anstruther. The Anstruther Fish Bar is probably the most well known and it serves buttered, white bread with your lunch and a metal tea pot. That's all you need to know! It's great!

3 Walk through Anstruther, sticking to the coast, and look for Fife Coastal Trail signs again. This time you'll pass through Pittenweem, old salt works and pass an outdoor swimming pool.

4 When you arrive in St. Monans - take some time to walk to the end of the harbour. Great for a photo at sunset!

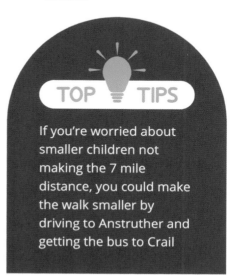

TOP TIPS

If you're worried about smaller children not making the 7 mile distance, you could make the walk smaller by driving to Anstruther and getting the bus to Crail

West Lomond Hill

SUMMARY

A circular walk on West Lomond Hill in Fife, exploring a hermit's cave and a mushroom-shaped rock.

START POINT

📍 KY14 7RR

🚌 Moffat Buses No. 95

🅿️ Bunnet Stane, free car park

📱 Scan below to download route

WEST LOMOND HILL

MIDI ADVENTURE

Difficulty	Easy - Medium
Distance	9 km
Location	Gateside (45 mins drive from Edinburgh)
Walk Type	Circular
Ascent	384 metres
What to Pack	Hiking boots Water bottle Picnic

RATINGS

Scenery	▬▬▬
Fun Factor	▬▬▬
Dog Suitability	▬▬▬
Public Toilets	▬

GETTING TO THE START

Nearest postcode for the starting point is KY14 7RR.
Once you have entered Gateside, turn left at Station Road and follow the road to its end (approximately three quarters of a mile). Turn right here and after a very short distance you will see the signs for 'The Bunnet Stane'.

There is a very small car park at the side of the road which only has space for about 5 vehicles. If the car park is full, keep driving for about 1-2km and there's more parking.

PUBLIC TRANSPORT

Get the Perth train from Edinburgh Waverly and get off at Ladybank.

Walk to the bus stop on Pitlessie Road and get the 66 to Kinross. Stay on the bus for about 20 minutes (22 stops!) and get off at the Primary School in Gateside. It's a short walk to the start from there.

HIGHLIGHTS

- **The Maiden Bower Cave:** You can get inside this cave and have a look around. It's very close to the Bunnet Stane.

- **The Bunnet Stane:** A rock formation close to the start of the walk that it looks like a giant mushroom.

- **Incredible Views:** At various parts of this walk, you'll see fantastic views of Loch Leven, Ochils, Arthur's Seat, Bass Rock and most of Fife.

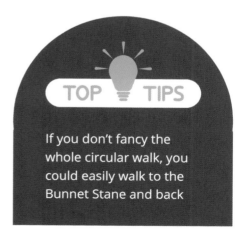

TOP TIPS

If you don't fancy the whole circular walk, you could easily walk to the Bunnet Stane and back

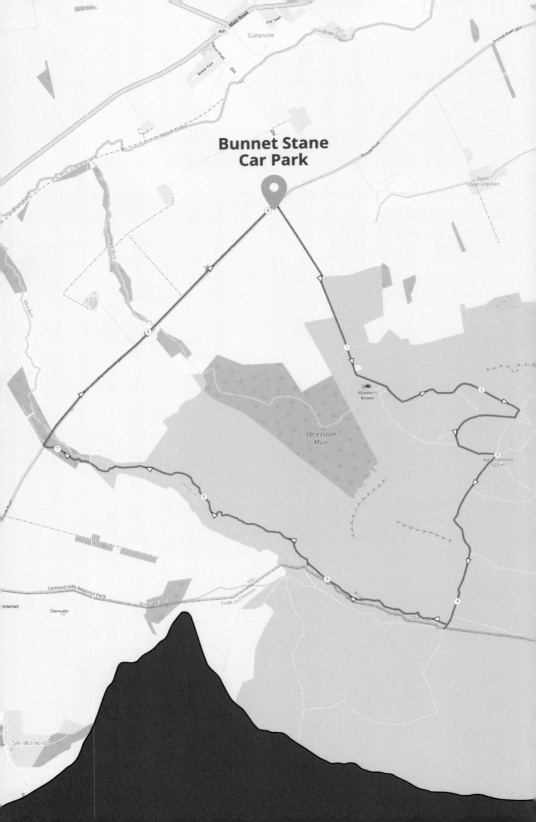

Bunnet Stane
Car Park

Gateside

Main Road

A91

Old Town

River Eden

Dryside Road Q57

Station Road

Bunet Park

Easter
Upper Urquhart

Dryside Road

River Eden

River Eden

Glen Burn

Glen Burn

Lacesston
Muir

Maiden's
Bower

West Lomond
522 m

Glen Burn

Edle

Lomond Hills Regional Park

Burnod Way

Perth and Kinross

Glenvale

Glenlomond

WALK DESCRIPTION

1 From the Bunnet Stane car park, follow the grassy track between fields.

2 The mushroom stone will eventually become clear in your view, you'll finally pass through a gate and head up through the grassy field to the Bunnet Stane

3 After the Bunnet Stane and head up to the top left corner of the field. Follow a path that continues to climb uphill diagonally across the slope to the left.

4 Cross a stile and keep going up! It will get steep here - keep going... Eventually the path meets the main path. At this junction, turn sharp right along this much clearer path.

5 Soon after the path splits with a steeper route heading directly for the summit.

Continue on the main track to the right as this gives a gentler ascent with better views and the direct path is causing erosion. Look out for the large cairn, which signals the summit.

6 Follow a grassy path towards Loch Leven (south west direction) and eventually reaches a stile over a stone wall. Cross this and follow the faint path down to a clearer path that runs to the left. It will be a bit boggy, but eventually meets the main path running from the Harper Lees reservoir to Glen Vale.

7 Turn right down this main path and down through Glen Vale to the footbridge, a small patch of woodland and eventually a tarmac lane. Turn right along this lane to return to the start.

Innerleithen to Peebles

Midi
Adventure

SUMMARY

This easy, largely flat cycle of 21km along an old railway track is a fantastic day out in Innerleithen, with a variety of landmarks to keep the adventure exciting.

START POINT

📍 EH44 6RD

🚌 Borders Bus No. X62

🅿️ Traquir Rd, Innerleithen

📱 Scan below to download route

INNERLEITHEN TO PEEBLES

MIDI ADVENTURE

Difficulty	Easy
Distance	21 km
Location	Innerleithen (1 hour drive from Edinburgh)
Cycle Type	There and back
Ascent	85 metres
What to Pack	Bike Helmet Water bottle Picnic

RATINGS

Scenery	▬▬▬
Fun Factor	▬▬▬
Dog Suitability	▬▬
Public Toilets	▬▬▬

GETTING TO THE START

Nearest postcode for the starting point is EH44 6RD, which is a one hour drive from Edinburgh. You'll pass through the village of Innerleithen. We highly recommend No. 1 Peebles Road Coffee House for delicious sandwiches, cakes and coffees. From the centre of Innerleithen, take the B709 down Traquir Road, passed the Traquir Arms Hotel and park around 200m down that road. You'll see the old railway path on your right. There's blue signposts marking the path for Cardrona and Peebles. Street parking here is free and this is where you should park up and get your bikes organised.

PUBLIC TRANSPORT

Borders Bus X62 for Peebles leaves the Edinburgh Bus Station every hour. After one hour and 40 minutes, you'll reach Innerleithen High Street. It's a short walk to the start from there.

HIGHLIGHTS

- **Cardrona Pumptrack:** Found 4km from the start of this adventure, on the outskirts of Cardrona. We encouraged our kids to be daredevils. After our turn, we realised it's terrifying!

- **Neidpath Tunnel:** Nearly half a mile long and pretty dark! It takes guts to cycle into this abyss...

- **Horsbrugh Castle Ruins:** At 6.5km the path forks and it's worth taking a quick detour to the right to explore the ruins of Horsbrugh Castle.

TOP TIPS

You may feel that you deserve an ice cream after this adventure. Cadwell's Luxury Ice Cream on Innerleithen High Street is highly recommended.

CYCLE DESCRIPTION

1 From Traquir Road in Innerleithen, look for the blue signs for Cardrona and Peebles.

2 The path is very well signposted for the whole adventure.

3 After 3km, you'll cross over the River Tweed and will pass lots of benches along the way.

4 In Cardrona, you'll cycle along the roads of a quiet housing estate. The road gets a little more daunting for younger kids at the roundabout and it's a good idea to keep a close eye on them here.

5 It's a straightforward cycle path for the next 5km, passing by Horsbrugh Castle and the Neidpath Tunnel. When complete, turn round and follow the path back to the start.

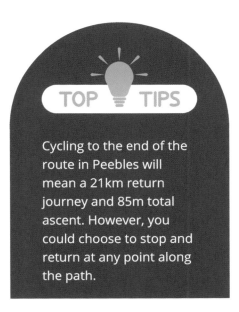

TOP TIPS

Cycling to the end of the route in Peebles will mean a 21km return journey and 85m total ascent. However, you could choose to stop and return at any point along the path.

Holy Island (Lindisfarne)

SUMMARY

Embrace the mud on this easy walk across the causeway following Pilgrim's Way to the Holy Island. Explore Lindisfarne and return by bus before the tide comes in!

START POINT

📍 TD15 2PB

🚌 X18 Max Arriva

🅿️ Lindisfarne Causeway

📱 Scan below to download route

HOLY ISLAND (LINDISFARNE)

MIDI ADVENTURE

Difficulty	Easy
Distance	8.5 km
Location	Holy Island (85 mins drive from Edinburgh)
Walk Type	A → B
Ascent	41 metres
What to Pack	Towel Wet Wipes Muddy Shoes Water

RATINGS

Scenery
Fun Factor
Dog Suitability
Public Toilets

Welcome to
HOLY ISLAND
Please use the visitors'
car park and help
protect our village.

GETTING TO THE START

This walk starts on the cross-section between the Northumberland Coastal Path and the Lindisfarne causeway on the mainland, just outside the village of Beal. The best postcode for this starting point is TD15 2PB. If you're driving, you'll want to park the car in the layby (on the left) at the causeway end, with space for around 7 cars. It's about 100 metres before the weatherbeaten refuge on stilts ahead of you!

PUBLIC TRANSPORT

It's relatively easy to get here on public transport and should take you around 90 minutes from Edinburgh Waverly.

Get a train to Berwick Upon Tweed. Then get the X18 Max Arriva North East bus. Stay on this for 22 stops and get off just after Haggerston Holiday Park.

The start of the walk is about 20 minutes from the bus stop.

HIGHLIGHTS

- **Pilgrim's Way:** This is signposted by poles and refuges across the causeway. It is the best route to walk to the island. It should take around 90 minutes. Only walk on a receding tide, barefoot and/or with waterproof shoes.

- **Lindisfarne Harbour and Castle:** Walk past the old upturned herring boats towards the castle. It's a lovely way to get a feel for the island

- **Pilgrim's Coffee House:** Family-run roasters on the island, with outdoor seating and great coffee.

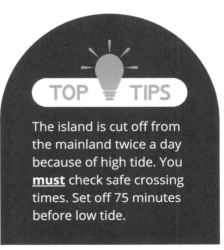

TOP TIPS

The island is cut off from the mainland twice a day because of high tide. You **must** check safe crossing times. Set off 75 minutes before low tide.

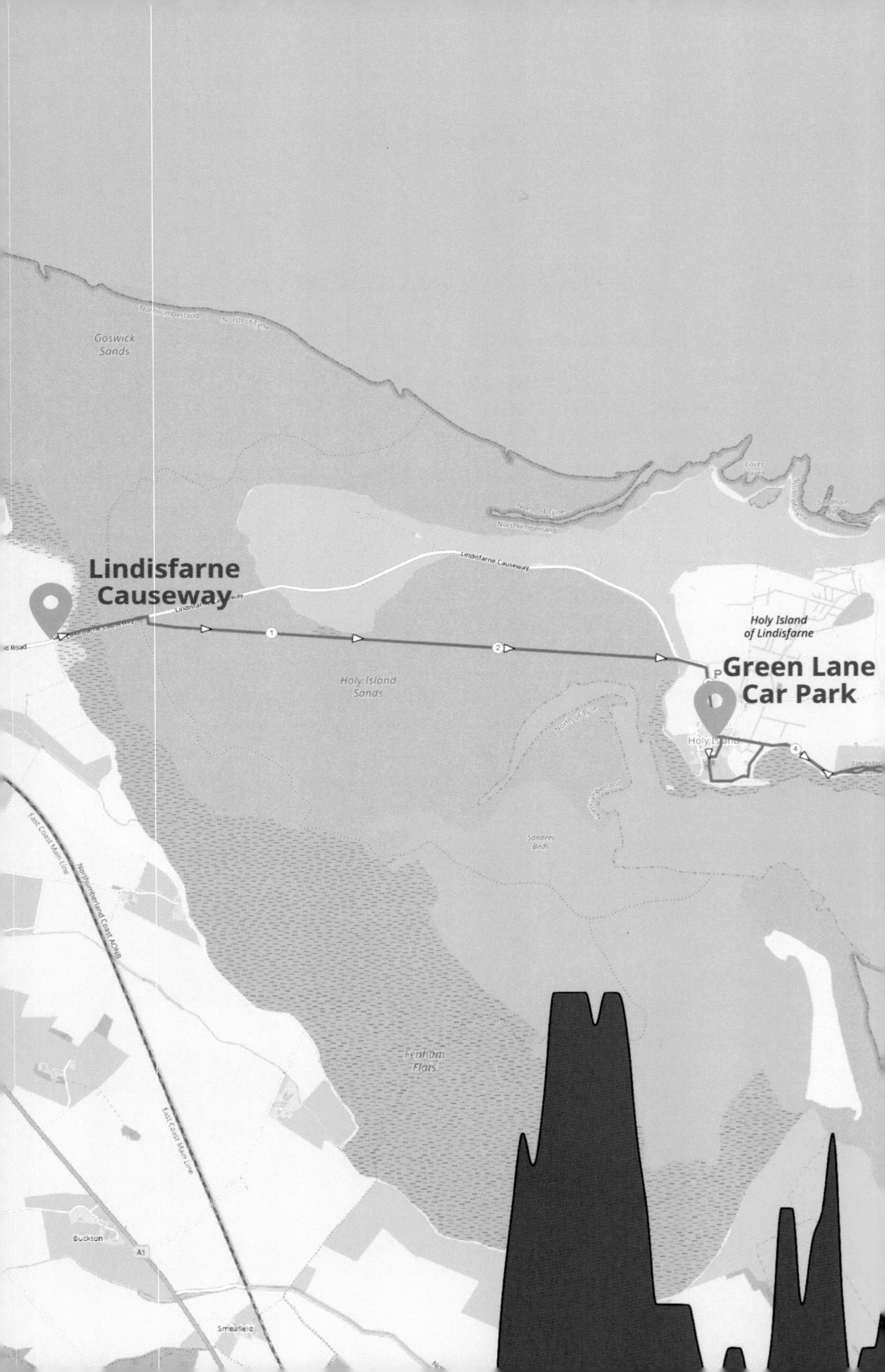

Lindisfarne Causeway
Green Lane Car Park
Goswick Sands
Northumberland
North of Tyne
Lindisfarne Causeway
Holy Island of Lindisfarne
Holy Island Sands
Holy Island
Coves Haven
Sandeel Beds
Fenham Flats
East Coast Main Line
Northumberland Coast AONB
Buckton
A1
Smeafield

WALK DESCRIPTION

1 Walk past the road bridge/causeway refuge. You'll cross over a small river.

2 After you've passed the refuge, look for the poles on your right - that's Pilgrim's Way. Step down onto the sand and follow the poles!

3 Parts of the walk can be muddy and wet. That's all part of the adventure! You can choose to skirt around these areas or whip your shoes off and tramp right through them.

4 The end of Pilgrim's Way is marked by a bench on the island. Holy Island village is only a 5 minute walk from here.

5 After exploring the island, we felt we had time to walk across the tarmac causeway back to the car. It was an easy(ish) walk. However, the bus is a good option too.

6 The 477 Borders Bus will take you back to the mainland, after you've walked across Pilgrim's Way. The timetable changes based on the tides. The bus leaves from the car park on Green Lane.

TOP TIPS

The walk across Pilgrim's Way is fun to do barefoot, especially in summer. It will save you having wet, soggy boots as you wander around the island.

Loch Leven

Midi
Adventure

SUMMARY

The Loch Leven Heritage Trail is a flat, traffic-free, gravel path circling the loch. It's a scenic and fun day out, with the opportunity to spot tonnes of wildlife.

START POINT

📍 KY13 9LY

🚌 Megabus to Kinross

🅿 RSPB Visitor Centre (Free)

📱 Scan below to download route

LOCH LEVEN

MIDI ADVENTURE

Difficulty	Easy
Distance	21 km
Location	Loch Leven RSPB Visitor Centre
Cycle Type	Circular
Ascent	100 metres
What to Pack	Bike Water bottle Snacks Cycle helmet

RATINGS

Scenery	▬▬▬▬
Fun Factor	▬▬▬▬
Dog Suitability	▬▬▬
Public Toilets	▬▬▬▬

GETTING TO THE START

Given that this is a circular route, you could really start anywhere. We have a car and began this adventure at the Loch Leven RSPB Visitor Centre. Another good place to start would be Kirkgate Park in Kinross.

Both starting points have free parking, cafe and toilets. It only take around 40 minutes to drive to both destinations from Edinburgh and both are located directly beside the circular heritage trail.

PUBLIC TRANSPORT

There's a Megabus to Kinross every hour from Edinburgh and it only takes around 50 minutes. It's easy to walk to Kirkgate Park from the bus drop off and you can begin the heritage trail from there.

HIGHLIGHTS

- **Kirkgate Park:** Located halfway around the trail, this park has swings, picnic benches, plenty of open space, a small beach area, and fantastic views looking out to Loch Leven

- **RSPB Visitor Centre:** Loch Leven nature reserve provides a haven for wildlife and attracts the largest concentration of ducks found anywhere in the UK with many thousands of migratory ducks, geese and swans every autumn and winter. The RSPB centre has an excellent viewing area upstairs with telescopes.

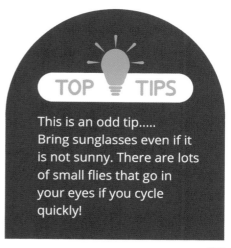

TOP TIPS

This is an odd tip.....
Bring sunglasses even if it is not sunny. There are lots of small flies that go in your eyes if you cycle quickly!

CYCLE DESCRIPTION

1 Go through the arch of the visitor centre and follow the path under the main road to the loch side

2 Turn left onto the heritage trail and you'll veer away from the loch for a while. You'll pass a covered lookout area and navigate the zig-zags.

3 Keep following the trail passed the cashmere mill and eventually you'll reach Kirkgate Park in Kinross.

4 From Kirkgate Park, look for the clear lochside gravel path (continuing in a clockwise direction around the loch). You'll pass a jetty, Fish Gate, Kinross House and eventually reach Mary's Gate.

5 Continue over the wooden bridge after Mary's Gate towards Burleigh Sands. Worth stopping here for a rest.

6 Keep following the signs for Findatie. The path soon enters the 'Black Woods' and meanders through the trees. Cross the bridge and turn right onto a road. You'll soon see the sluice building at Findatie come into view. Turn left here past a metal barrier and then immediately right. Stay on the main path to climb up to the end of the route (and back to the start!)

TOP TIPS

Shortly after Burliegh Sands, there is the chance to detour on a signed path to the award-winning Loch Leven Larder, a cafe and farm shop.

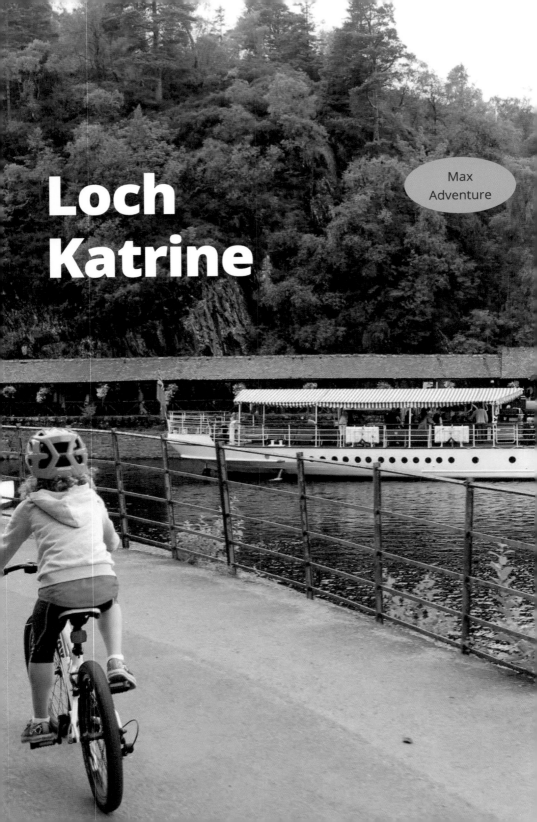

Loch Katrine

Max
Adventure

SUMMARY

Board the Sir Walter Scott Steam Boat with your bike and cycle back. Enjoy the travelling in the steam boat, and a 13-mile traffic free cycle - only 1 hour drive from Edinburgh

START POINT

📍 FK17 8HZ

🚌 Loch Katrine Cruises

🅿 Trossachs Pier (Paid)

📱 Scan below to download route

LOCH KATRINE

MAX ADVENTURE

Difficulty	Medium
Distance	21 km cycle
Location	Loch Katrine (1 hour drive from Edinburgh)
Cycle Type	A → B
Ascent	350 metres
What to Pack	Bike Water bottle Snacks Cycle helmet

RATINGS

Scenery	▬▬▬▬
Fun Factor	▬▬▬
Dog Suitability	▬▬▬
Public Toilets	▬▬

GETTING TO THE START

You're going to want to leave early. The boat sets sail around 10am and it takes about an hour to drive there from Edinburgh.

For those wanting to travel to Loch Katrine by car, access is via a spur road off the A821 at the end of Loch Achray. (POSTCODE: FK17 8HZ).

There is also a seasonal bus service operating along a circular route between Callander and Aberfoyle via the Trossachs Pier and a regular bus service between Stirling and Callander.

BIKE HIRE

If you don't want to travel to Loch Katrine with your bike, there are local hire facilities available at 'Katrinewheelz', part of the Trossachs Pier complex.
They have everything from children's bikes to tandems (and even electric bikes).

HIGHLIGHTS

- Steam Boat from The Trossachs Pier near Callander is a truly special experience.
- Bike Hire available from a shop next to the pier including e-bikes.
- Steam Boat takes you one hour to the end of Loch Katrine.
- Bikes are free to take on the boat and there is a snack bar on board.
- The road next to the loch is closed to traffic so the cycling is safe and stress-free.

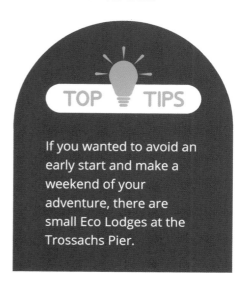

TOP TIPS

If you wanted to avoid an early start and make a weekend of your adventure, there are small Eco Lodges at the Trossachs Pier.

CYCLE DESCRIPTION

Although the cycle route is easy(ish), there ARE hills. However, we managed the whole 13 miles with kids aged around 7-9. It was really fun. Loads of places to stop for snacks.

1. After disembarking the steam boat at Stronachlachar Pier (quick stop at the cafe - if needed!), cycle up the road until you pass Hillview Cottage. Turn right after the cottage, go past a white gate and follow the road slightly downhill.

2. Follow the road, ignore a turning to the right and pass some houses and the road barrier.

3. This road basically continues for 13 miles! It is only open to local traffic and cyclists - so it's safe and peaceful.

4. You'll gradually follow the shore of Loch Katrine until you arrive back a Trossachs Pier.

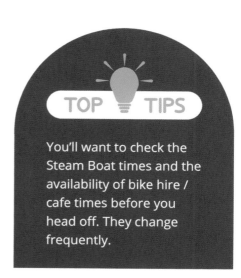

TOP TIPS

You'll want to check the Steam Boat times and the availability of bike hire / cafe times before you head off. They change frequently.

The Cobbler

Max Adventure

SUMMARY

The Cobbler is 884 metres high and located in Succoth. Really called Ben Arthur, but nicknamed the Cobbler, you'll enjoy the drama of the Arrochar Alps with insane views.

START POINT

📍 G83 7AP

🚌 Citylink No. 926

🅿 Succoth Car Park (Paid)

📱 Scan below to download route

THE COBBLER

MAX ADVENTURE

Difficulty	Medium
Distance	11 km
Location	Succouth (2 hours drive from Edinburgh)
Walk Type	There and back
Ascent	862 metres
What to Pack	Walking boots Water bottle Picnic Walking poles

RATINGS

Scenery	▬▬▬
Fun Factor	▬▬▬
Dog Suitability	▬▬▬
Public Toilets	▬

GETTING TO THE START

If driving, the starting point is the car park in the village of Succouth (Postcode: G83 7AP). It's a large car park but get's busy if you don't get there early. It's a nice drive from Edinburgh along the side of Loch Lomond.

Thankfully Arrochar is also straightforward to get to by bus or train.

The citylink bus service (number 926) runs several times a day between Glasgow and Arrochar and takes 1 hour and 10 minutes.

There are also a number of trains out of Glasgow Queens Street station direct to Arrochar. Again it's about a 1 hour 10 minute journey.

HIGHLIGHTS

- As you exit the forest after the first third of the walk, you get an amazing view of the Cobbler ahead of you. It's awesome!
- There are some really great rest spots on the walk: beside the river as you exit the forest, the Narnain boulders and the top of the Cobbler itself.
- There's a real sense of achievement when you reach the top of the Cobbler. The scenery helps!

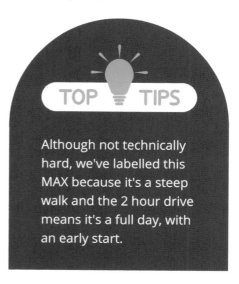

TOP TIPS

Although not technically hard, we've labelled this MAX because it's a steep walk and the 2 hour drive means it's a full day, with an early start.

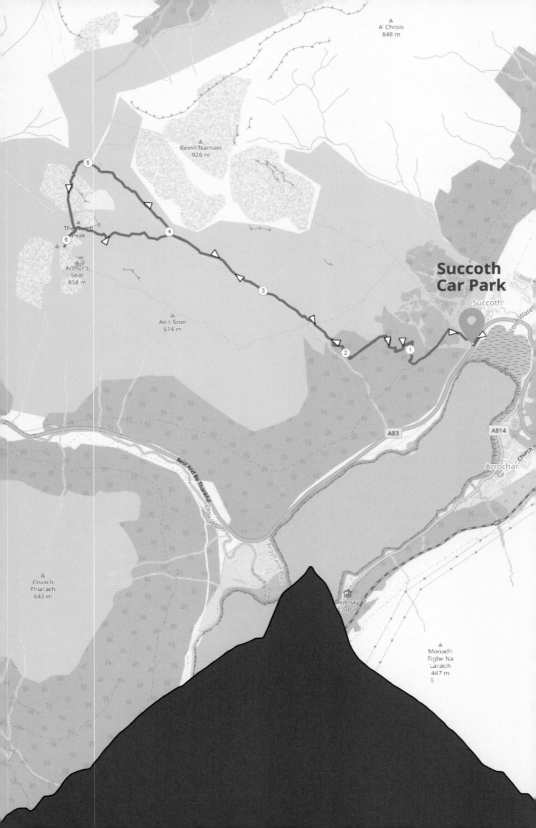

WALK DESCRIPTION

1 From the car park in Succouth, cross the road and you'll see a large notice board marking the start of the trail.

2 Climb up through the trees following the main path. The path zig zags steadily upwards for about an hour of walking. It's fairly gentle and when you look backwards the loch and a view of Ben Lomond starts to open up

3 After a final few turns the tree line ends and you enter a valley with the peak of the Cobbler in the distance in front of you.

4 Pass through the massive Narnain boulders that are either side of the path as you near the start of the exciting climbing ahead.

5 When a fork is reached, keep right and continue up the valley.

6 Shortly after a small lochan to your left, the path forks again. Turn left to start the steep climb up. There are steps pretty much the whole way up to the top. Enjoy the view!

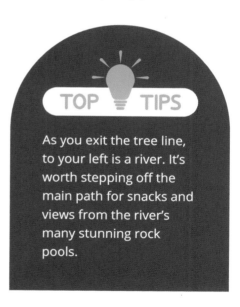

TOP TIPS

As you exit the tree line, to your left is a river. It's worth stepping off the main path for snacks and views from the river's many stunning rock pools.

One Day: West Highland Way

Max
Adventure

ONE DAY: WEST HIGHLAND WAY

SUMMARY

One of the best sections of the West Highland Way in one day; from Crianlarich to Bridge of Orchy. The train journey is a joy in itself and the scenery is stunning

START POINT

📍 PA36 4AD

🚌 Train from Glasgow

🅿 Bridge of Orchy train station (free)

📱 Scan below to download route

Difficulty	Medium
Distance	21 km
Location	Crianlarich to Bridge of Orchy
Walk Type	A → B
Ascent	495 metres
What to Pack	Walking boots Water bottle Picnic Walking poles

RATINGS

Scenery

Fun Factor

Dog Suitability

Public Toilets

GETTING TO THE START

The starting point is the Bridge of Orchy train station, where you'll catch the train to Crainlarich.

If you're driving there in the morning, you're going to want to leave early. Ideally catching the train from Bridge of Orchy to Crainlarich at 9am. This means leaving Edinburgh at 6:30am....!

There's a good car park in the train station and you can park there all day. The postcode is PA36 4AD.

Another alternative is to stay the night before in the Bridge of Orchy hotel the evening before. It's a great hotel with a variety of rooms at different price points.

If using public transport, you'll have to stay in the hotel the evening before. The hotel is directly across the road from the train station.

HIGHLIGHTS

- If you catch a clear, crisp day - you cannot beat the feeling of standing on the remote train station surrounded by beautiful hills.
- The walk encapsulates woodland, farmland, rivers, waterfalls, highland scenery, old graveyards, campsites and tourist village (Tyndrum). It's so varied. There are so many distractions to keep the whole family walking.

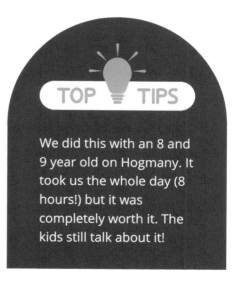

TOP TIPS

We did this with an 8 and 9 year old on Hogmany. It took us the whole day (8 hours!) but it was completely worth it. The kids still talk about it!

WALK DESCRIPTION

1 Park the car in Bridge of Orchy and jump on the train to Crianlarich. There is only one train each morning.

2 Cross the main road out of the station and you see a big sign for West Highland Way / Drovers Loop. Follow the path into the woods and after 5 minutes you join the main West Highland Way route.

3 The path out of Crianlarich takes you up hill into the woods high above the village. This is really the only major piece of uphill walking for the day.

4 The route passes through a gate to pass St Fillan's Priory There is an old graveyard on your left and you soon reach the Strathfillan Wigwams.

5 From there the path follows the river into Tyndrum, where you can grab lunch.

6 At the end of Tyndrum, take the road leading gently uphill next to the mini market. The route runs fairly parallel to the train track back to Bridge of Orchy.

TOP TIPS

This walk is a great introduction to walking the highlands. If you enjoy it as much as we did, the route from Bridge of Orchy to Glen Coe is just as amazing across Rannoch Moor.

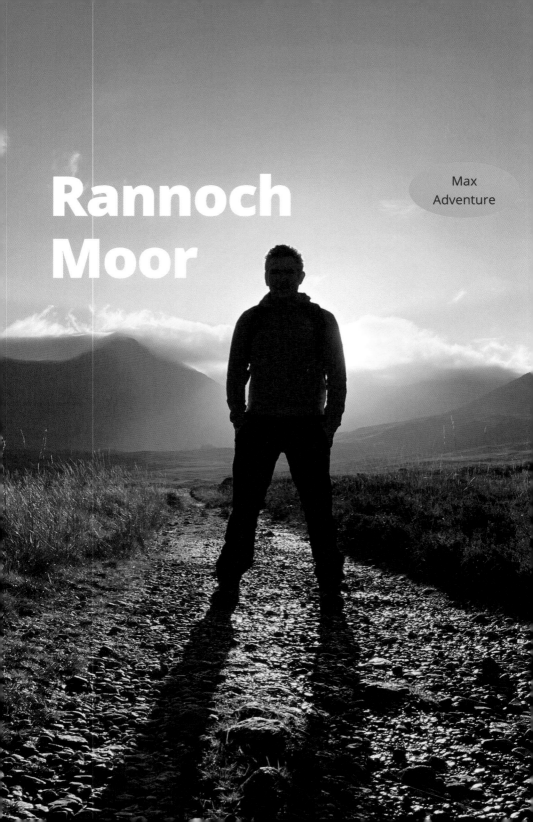

Rannoch Moor

Max Adventure

RANNOCH MOOR

SUMMARY

Hail down the bus at Glencoe Ski Centre. Hop off in Bridge of Orchy and follow the Military Road across Rannoch Moor landing back in the jaws of Glencoe

START POINT

📍 PH49 4HZ

🚌 Citylink 914 or 915

🅿️ Glencoe Ski Centre (free)

📱 Scan below to download route

Difficulty	Medium
Distance	17.5 km
Location	Bridge of Orchy to Glencoe Ski Centre
Walk Type	A → B
Ascent	499 metres
What to Pack	Walking boots Water bottle Picnic Walking poles

RATINGS

Scenery	▰▰▰▰ ▰
Fun Factor	▰▰▰ ▰
Dog Suitability	▰▰▰
Public Toilets	▰▰▰

GETTING TO THE START

The starting point is the Glencoe Ski Centre (POSTCODE: PH49 4HZ). There's a free car park here, decent toilets and a cafe.

From here, walk down the White Corries Road to the A82 and flag down the Citylink bus to Bridge of Orchy. There's no evidence of a bus stop, but you can easily flag the bus down.

If you're driving there in the morning, you're going to want to leave early. It's a 3 hour drive (and super worth it!)

Alternatively, you could stay the night in either the Bridge of Orchy Hotel or Kingshouse Hotel. They are both lovely places to stay.

If using public transport, you'll have to stay in the Bridge of Orchy hotel the evening before. The hotel is directly across the road from the Bridge of Orchy train station. Easy!

HIGHLIGHTS

- The walk starts beside Black Rock Cottage, one of the most photographed buildings in Scotland. With Glen Etive towering behind, it's the perfect base for the Ladies' Scottish Climbing Club.

- The bus journey is a joy in itself. The excitement of making sure you flag the bus down will keep the kids on their toes!

TOP TIPS

Keep your eye on your weather app to choose the best day possible for this. This is a longish day out and worth avoiding the rain for.

Glencoe Ski Centre

Bridge of Orchy

WALK DESCRIPTION

1 This day out makes for an early start if you are starting in Edinburgh. The drive is just under 3 hours. We left at 6.30am and had enough time to grab a morning roll and coffee at the Glencoe Ski Centre before flagging down the bus to Bridge of Orchy.

2 After hopping off the bus at Bridge or Orchy, head over the bridge behind the hotel. Follow the road briefly and then immediately left onto a signed footpath that climbs up to a gate and enters the forestry.

3 Eventually the path levels off and then descends to the Inverornan Hotel. Join the road as it veers round to the right, over a bridge and passed a small wild camping area. The road ends at the Forest Lodge.

4 Go straight ahead at the Forest Lodge, pass through a gate and join the military road. Initially walking up a slight incline, with forestry around you, you'll eventually open out into the vast wilderness of Rannoch Moor.

5 Follow this road all the way to Glencoe Ski Centre. Eventually you'll spot Glen Etive in the distance and Black Rock cottage ahead of you. At this stage, you head slightly back up the hill to the car park.

TOP TIPS

This is a super remote walk. There is one hotel on the route that doesn't cater for non-residents. Please make sure you bring enough food!

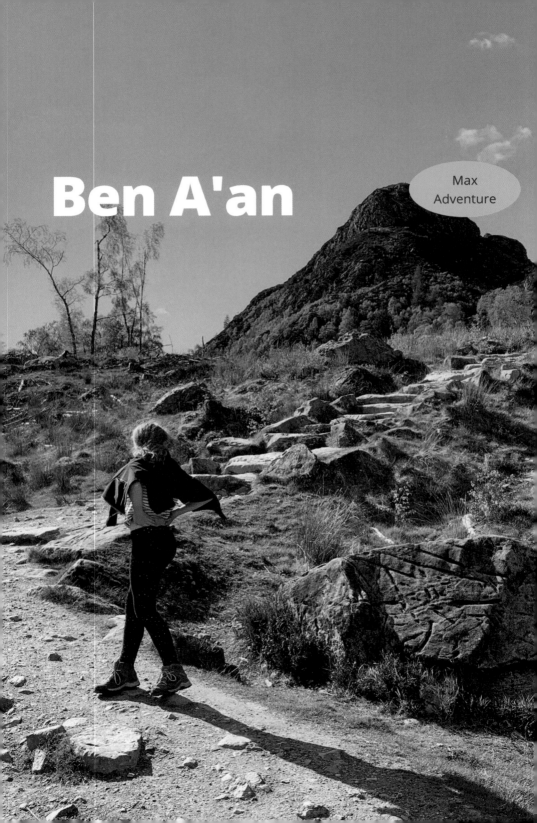

Ben A'an

Max
Adventure

SUMMARY

Famously known as the mountain in miniature in the Trossachs, Ben A'an is an easy hill that has all the benefits of a true mountain climb, but easier on the legs!

START POINT

📍 FK17 8HY

🅿 Ben A'an Car Park

📱 Scan below to download route

BEN A'AN

MAX ADVENTURE

Difficulty	Easy / Medium
Distance	3.7 km
Location	Loch Achray (90 mins drive from Edinburgh)
Walk Type	There and back
Ascent	348 metres
What to Pack	Hiking Boots Water Snacks Walking Poles

RATINGS

Scenery	▬▬▬▬
Fun Factor	▬▬▬▬
Dog Suitability	▬▬▬
Public Toilets	▪

GETTING TO THE START

If driving, the starting point is the Ben A'an car park beside Loch Achray on the A821 from Kilmahog to Loch Katrine (Postcode: FK17 8HY).

It's a large, but busy car park. Our experience has been to either arrive very early in the day or, given that the walk only take a few hours, later in the afternoon once others have finished and the car park clears slightly.

PUBLIC TRANSPORT

It's not easy to get here by public transport... There is a seasonal bus called the Trossachs Trundler that operates between Callander and Aberfoyle. Contact the Tourist Information at Loch Katrine for information on this.

WILDLIFE WATCH

You might spot native roe and red deer amongst the trees. We climbed on a calm, clear day in May and were fascinated to see a Golden Eagle soar above us. It was HUGE!

HIGHLIGHTS

- Ben A'an is famously called the Trossachs 'Mountain in Miniature". It's perfect for little legs to experience a true mountains climb without the pain of a full day hike.

- You can see as far as Loch Lomond from the panoramic views at the top.

TOP TIPS

Many websites advise that you arrive early to ensure a parking space. We actually went mid-late afternoon and it was fine. Don't park on the road verge - you'll get fined! If you arrive and there's no space, head over to Trossachs Pier and spend some time there.

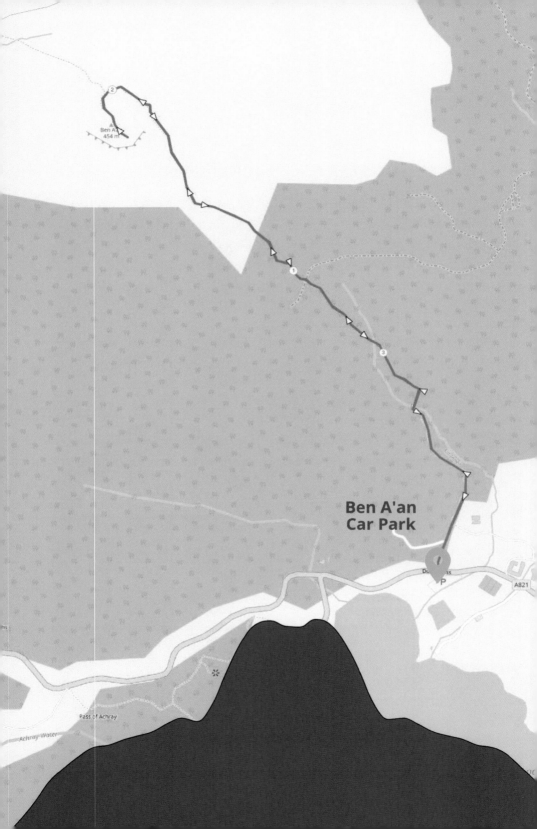

Ben A'an
454 m

**Ben A'an
Car Park**

A821

WALK DESCRIPTION

Despite being a small walk in length, we've labelled this a MAX adventure due to the distance from Edinburgh.

1. Cross the road from the car park and follow the signposted path for Ben A'an. There's an increasing incline towards the trees.

2. Cross the footbridge and follow the river up the hill. You'll navigate the stepping stones across the river again and the view will start to open up. Eventually you'll see the sharp point of Ben A'an ahead of you.

3. The incline levels off and you'll feel like you're walking across moorland. Eventually the path veers right and you have to start the rock-climbing section of the walk!

4. Keep climbing up the hill. The path swoops around the back of Ben A'an with a few more rocks to climb before you reach the summit.

5. Once at the top, the landscape makes for a perfect backdrop to a victory photograph!

TOP TIPS

This adventure pairs perfectly with the Loch Katrine adventure on the next page. Why not stay in the Loch Katrine ecolodges and make a weekend of it?

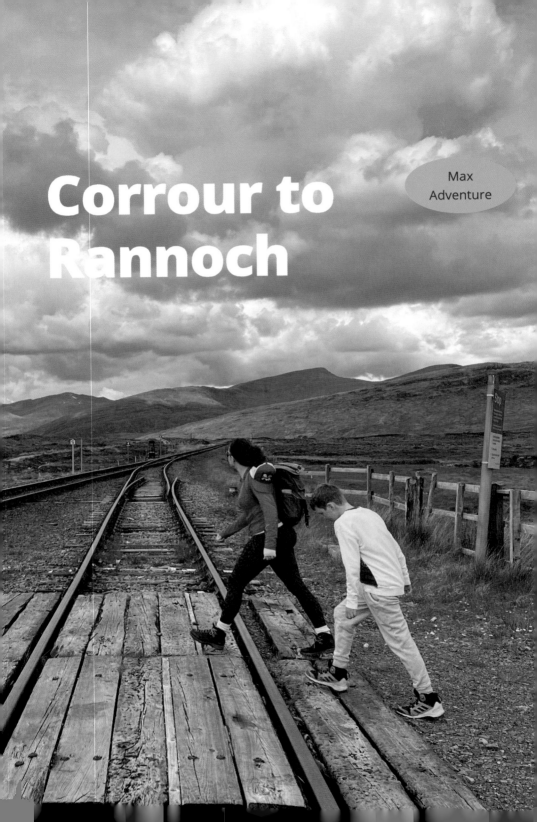

Corrour to Rannoch

Max
Adventure

SUMMARY

Trek along the Road to the Isles from Corrour to Rannoch Station, and make use of the most remote train station in the UK, made famous in Trainspotting

START POINT

📍 PH17 2QA

🚌 Train from Glasgow

🅿 Rannoch train station (free)

📱 Scan below to download route

CORROUR TO RANNOCH

MAX ADVENTURE

Difficulty	Medium - Hard
Distance	18 km
Location	Rannoch Station (2 hours drive from Edinburgh)
Walk Type	A → B
Ascent	224 metres
What to Pack	Walking boots Water bottle Snacks

RATINGS

Scenery	▬▬▬▬
Fun Factor	▬▬▬▬
Dog Suitability	▬▬▬
Public Toilets	▬▬▬

GETTING TO THE START

Rannoch Station is one of the most remote railway stations in the British Isles located approx 16 miles from the village of Kinloch Rannoch.

If you're driving there in the morning, you're going to want to leave early; ideally catching the train from Rannoch to Corrour at 11am. This means leaving Edinburgh at 7:30-8am....

There's a good car park in the train station and you can park there all day for free. The postcode is PH17 2QA.

Another alternative is to travel there by train the day before and stay in the area. There are a couple of highly rated camping pods / cabins at Rannoch Station. Best way to find these is to type "Rannoch Station" into an AirBnb search.

INSECT ALERT

Beware of sunny days with no wind! That's when horseflies and midges will strike.

HIGHLIGHTS

- Catch the train to Corrour (the most remote in the UK), which featured in the famous trainspotting scene and don't miss out on the Corrour cafe. It is truly fantastic.
- Take a small detour at Loch Ossian to explore the Youth Hostel there. Super cute and can sleep 36 people!
- The route follows the Road to the Isles. The shallow ascent at the start becomes mostly downhill after 6km.

TOP TIPS

There are good toilets at Rannoch Station and a lovely tearoom. Great for a quick coffee before catching the train.

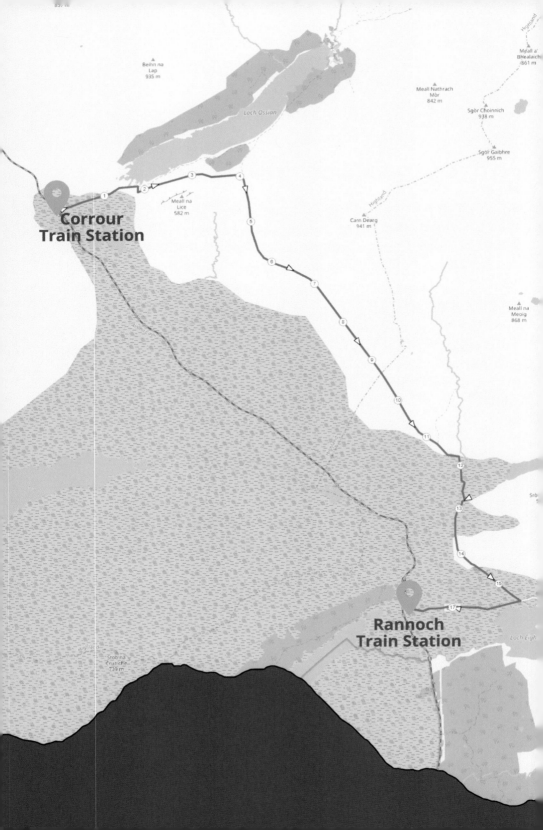

WALK DESCRIPTION

1 Park the car in the Rannoch Station free car park. There are good public toilets there and a lovely tearoom for a coffee and cake. Jump on the train to Corrour. There is only one train each morning - so check train times in advance and make sure you don't miss it! The train takes 12 minutes and you pay for your ticket on the train, with the conductor.

2 Upon arriving at Corrour train station, it's worth taking the obligatory Trainspotting photo and visiting the cafe in the station house. Follow the track for Corrour Youth Hostel and Rannoch.

3 Follow the road until you see the Corrour Youth Hostel on your left, beside Loch Ossian. At this stage, look for signs for "Rannoch Road".

4 This is the Road to the Isles and your route back to the car. Follow the road for 15km.

5 Eventually, you'll come to the end of the Road to the Isles track and intersect with the B846. Walk the final 2km back to the car.

TOP TIPS

On the drive home from this mammoth walk, we parked on the banks of Loch Rannoch and went for a paddle. It was so refreshing and just what our tired feet needed!

135

PICNICS AND PRINGLES

We try to save money by packing a picnic for our adventures. We're big fans of Pringles, especially Salt & Vinegar or Prawn Cocktail flavour. We'll never forget the disastrous Pentlands trip where we got to the top of the hill and realised we'd bought Honey Glazed Ham Pringles instead of Prawn Cocktail. Needless to say, we did not include that particular adventure in this book. Too many bad memories!

After we'd finished writing this book, we counted Pringles featuring in six of our adventures in this book.

Can you spot the Pringles in six of our adventures?

P.S. We're not sponsored by Pringles (sadly!) - we just love them.

137

FREQUENTLY ASKED QUESTIONS

 Do we need hiking boots?

It's probably best. There's nothing worse than having wet feet for hours. You don't have to buy expensive ones. For adults, the lowest priced boot would probably be Peter Storm boots from Go Outdoors. If you can afford a little more, then Jack Wolfskin, Merrell and Scarpa boots are good. Sally has Arc'Teryx boots and they're not as good as the old Scarpa ones she had.

Kids hiking boots can often be 'hand me downs'. If you're looking to buy new, then we highly recommend Adidas Terrex hiking boots. They come in around £50-£70. You can always sell them on once they grow out of them.

 How do you get kids to walk without complaining?

Our kids definitely complained the first few walks. We used a couple of tricks to get them motivated.... here they are:

1. Walk with friends. They complain *waaaaaay* less when they are distracted by friends.
2. Give them ownership of their favourite snacks. We discovered this one by just getting annoyed with them constantly asking for snacks. We put the snacks in their pockets and instantly less complaining.
3. Let them take photos. Tell them they can send the photos to family, friends, school after the walk.
4. Find distractions on the walk.
   a. Who can find the biggest shell on the beach?
   b. Who will be the first to see a sheep, cow, plane, etc?
   c. Name 20 different types of chocolate bar / board game / bird / farm animal / country

FREQUENTLY ASKED QUESTIONS

3 **What should we pack?**

- A couple of bottles of water
- Picnic and snacks
- One pair of dry socks
- Waterproof jackets for everyone
- Hats and gloves for everyone

4 **How do you find these places?**

Dan spends a lot of time on instagram!

Also, WalkTheHighlands website is great for describing walks in more detail.

The challenge we have found is that most good walks have been so well publicised that they have become too busy. Have you ever tried to park at Flotterstone in the Pentlands on a sunny day? The adventures included in this book have the 'wow' factor of the best of Scotland, but don't include the overcrowding.

EDINBURGH
ADVENTURES

If you've enjoyed an Edinburgh Adventure, why not tag us on Instagram and show us how much fun you've had!

@edinburgh_adventures

mcdonald_nj Thanks @edinburgh_adventures for the inspiration!

jacqueline.c.lamont Amazing walk up West Lomond Hill today. Thank you @edinburgh_adventures !!

Printed in Poland
by Amazon Fulfillment
Poland Sp. z o.o., Wrocław
28 July 2022

e1dbd5bb-0450-4fb6-a418-0d173eea567eR01